For those who have stayed,

those who are gone,

and

those who have been left behind.

# Forever Changed
## by

# Suicide

# Acknowledgements

Thank you to each of the authors who have contributed to this book. Thank you for sharing your thoughts, your pain, your journeys. It has not been easy, but I thank you for your courage.

Thank you, Penny Hayes, for the beautiful poem. It speaks to so much of what this book is about.

Thank you to my husband, Peter, who has been with me on this journey, on so many journeys in the past, and hopefully, many more journeys to come. You are the wind beneath my wings.

Thank you to the most awesome publisher, Deborah Fay. I really appreciate your support and feedback.

Most of all, for Craig Allan Springsteen, our son, thank you for the time you shared with us. I remember each and every moment with joy as I share a little of your story here.

Thank you also to you, the reader. May you find comfort, peace and connection within the stories and with each of the authors in this book. I hope that these stories resonate with you, help you understand those who have been on this journey, and maybe shine a light for you if you are currently on this journey yourself. Through reading, you become a part of our stories. There are details at the end of most chapters if you wish to connect with the author.

# CONTENT WARNING

The stories within contain descriptions of
topics such as suicide, the handling of
cadavers, self-harm, drug and alcohol abuse,
domestic violence, and sexual abuse (of both
adults and children).

Some of these stories may be triggering.
If you have been impacted by any of these,
please contact your local support group or any
of the groups in the resources section at the
end of this book. Reach out and speak to a
friend, family member or support person.

# Forever Changed by Suicide

For those who have stayed,

those who are gone,

and

those who have been left behind.

Compilation by
Trish Springsteen

**Forever Changed by Suicide**

Compiled by Trish Springsteen

Copyright 2020 Trish Springsteen
          4 Light Place
          Caboolture South QLD
          Australia 4510

First published by Disruptive Publishing, 2021

Disruptive Publishing
          17 Spencer Avenue
          Deception Bay QLD 4508
          www.disruptivepublishing.com.au
          deb@disruptivepublishing.com.au

If you or someone you know is feeling suicidal, please reach out for assistance. See the resources section in the back of the book for details of various support agencies.

ISBN: 978-0-6487451-1-2

# Table of Contents

# The Extent of My Grief

My numbness is a measure of how much

I can't bear to think of your death.

The extent of my huge anger marks

how much I wish you hadn't done it.

The tears flowing down my cheeks

paint trails of sadness

and the story of how much I miss you.

The bargaining I try to make and all those what ifs,

shows how desperate I am to have you back

and the loneliness I have.

And when acceptance comes as it does in time,

I will at last calm down and feel you there,

forever in the centre of my heart,

where I continue to talk to you,

and cuddle you in my arms of love.

*Penny Hayes © July 2020*

# I Remember

## Trish Springsteen

*I sit here today remembering – 13 years ago today. I remember it was a normal day … I remember the first inkling of something being wrong in the afternoon… I remember breaking that door down… I remember finding our son gone from this earth, WHY … I remember fragments of that evening that night … I remember the agonised cry from my husband, his father … I remember a loving boy, Craig … I remember holding him in my arms when he was born … I remember him growing up a cheeky, loving boy … I remember him so excited when he was Dux of his primary school … I remember a handsome caring young man … I remember so many lovely moments … I remember and cherish all those memories – the sweet, the bitter – because they are what makes up our son …*

On the 3rd of October 2007, our lives changed forever. The day started normally, and I woke up to a bright day at home. I was off duty from work and had settled down to work on my own business, Trischel. It was the early days of the business and I was still working full time as well as slowly getting Trischel up and running.

There was no indication at that time of how that day was going to end.

We were a family of four: Peter and me, and our two children, Rochelle and Craig. A normal family with the usual ups and downs but nothing that stood out as a wake-up call of what was to come.

We had been living in Brisbane since 1989, having moved from Canberra where Rochelle and Craig had been born. I grew up and went to school in Canberra, and had four very close friends. It was while I was studying in Melbourne that I met Peter. Peter was born and grew up in Melbourne. We met, and after a year, we got engaged. Peter moved to Canberra and then a year later, in 1976, we married. I was twenty, and Peter was twenty-eight. We had our whole lives ahead of us.

Rochelle came along in 1981, followed by Craig in 1984. There was going to be more, however two caesareans and life got in the way. We were happy because we had a girl and a boy. It was just right.

Craig was going to be named Jonathon right up until the night before he was born, when he became Craig. It just seemed right. It really confused his grandmother, my mum, as we hadn't had time to tell her. It worked for us though. Peter means rock, Rochelle means little rock, and Craig was rocky crag. Me, well, I was the Noble Lady bringing everyone together.

Life moved on. Craig had just started preschool when a trip to Brisbane for the 1988 World Expo, and the increasing cold winds off the Snowy Mountains in Canberra, convinced us to move to Brisbane. It was a quick decision. We visited in September 1988, and moved to Brisbane in January 1989.

We settled into the Brisbane phase of our family life. It took time to make some new friends, but they came. The move had been early enough that Rochelle and Craig settled well into school and life in Brisbane. We started out at Bald Hills. Both Rochelle and Craig went to Bald Hills Primary School, then Rochelle moved on to Aspley High School and to University for a very short time before moving overseas to Orange County, California. That's another story, but it was ultimately a good move for her. She married and is living there now. It was difficult not having her around, and only keeping in touch via Skype. Craig was nearby though, and growing up into a lovely, handsome, caring young man.

I remember Craig as a baby and holding him in my arms – a boy to carry on the Springsteen name, and such a happy, mischievous boy with a cheeky grin. Craig and Rochelle had a normal brother-sister relationship and became very close, always looking after each other. They were both so very much loved.

I remember Craig as a good student. He'd decided in his final year at Bald Hills Primary School that he wanted to be Dux of the school, the top academic student for the year. He told me at the beginning of the year that was his goal. He said to me that he had told his teachers at the school that that was what he wanted to do. "Go for it!" I said, "It's a great goal." I actually never thought he would do it, but I hoped for him and supported him. It was such a high goal. Well, he did it. Dux of Bald Hills Primary School was our son Craig. We were so very proud of him. His name is there inscribed on their shield hanging in the reception area. I didn't realise at the time how very much that was going to mean to me.

I remember Craig growing into a handsome man and going to Caboolture High School, coping with the change to the high school environment. He was still a good student, finding his way, making friends, a seemingly normal teenager growing up.

I remember Craig joining Demolay, which was part of Freemasons for young men. Such a great organisation, teaching young men leadership, caring, work ethic and community involvement. A very large part of Craig's life was in connecting to so many friends. Craig made friends easily, and he connected to so many people in so many areas of his life.

I remember Craig never missing a Mother's Day and going out for brunch. He never forgot Mother's or Father's Day.

I remember our chats on the phone. I remember having to stand on the stair above him, he had gotten so tall, so that I could look him in the eye when I was trying to tell him off, which usually ended up in laughter. I couldn't keep a straight face.

I remember Craig and his first girlfriend – the girls that were his friends. I remember how awesome he looked in a suit, and what a sought-after escort he was for the Deb Balls.

I remember Craig finishing High School, being unsure of what he wanted to do. He had gotten entry to some University units that he completed whilst in the final year at high school. He was going to be a forensic psychologist, maybe a criminologist, maybe a psychologist, an entrepreneur, a disc jockey. There were so many choices, and so many options for him to explore.

I remember Craig getting his first job, working in technology, coming to work with me at my work so that he could work from home whilst studying.

I remember Craig living at home with us, then going out to live with his girlfriend, then coming back home, then going to live in flat of his own.

It's coming – we are here – I remember that day that changed everything.

We woke up that morning to a beautiful day, a family of four: Peter and I at home in Bald Hills, Rochelle in America, Craig in his flat at Newstead.

We went to bed that night changed forever – Peter and I at home in Bald Hills, Rochelle in America – Craig gone; gone from the flat at Newstead – gone from our lives forever, gone from this life.

The 3rd of October 2007 lives on in my memory. I can't forget that day. It blurs, but there are snapshots that stand out and will always stand out in my memory. The question is always there – WHY? – there is no answer. There were no indications, no hints that there was trouble.

I remember it started around midday – 1pm. Craig was working from home, and I got a call saying that he couldn't be reached. I tried to call him on the phone, but he was not answering. I was worried, but not too worried. I thought he may be sick and couldn't reach his phone. I had to take over his shift, as there was work to be done. I couldn't leave home to go and see him, and I couldn't reach him. That niggling feeling was getting bigger and bigger. He must be sick. Finally, the shift ended, and Peter and I were in the car, on the way to his flat. I had called a friend of his to meet us there.

I remember arriving, meeting his friend. We couldn't get in and he was not answering the phone or the door. It must have been around 5.30pm to 6pm. Time starts to blur.

I remember breaking down that damn door. We just broke it. I remember seeing him there hanging! It could not be true – it could not be true. I remember getting him down. I remember Peter saying no, no, don't do this.

I remember starting CPR, but it was too late, he was cold, but we had to try. I am breathing for my baby; my child why isn't he breathing for himself? I am crying, I am devastated and time blurs.

I remember calling an ambulance and throwing the phone at his friend to speak to them because I couldn't remember the street address. What did an address mean when Craig was gone?

I remember calling my mum and wondering, how do I tell her that her grandson is gone? They were on the way to the airport and my stepfather was flying out to work. They came to the flat instead.

I remember calling my friend to say I can't come to the meeting now because our son is gone.

I remember Peter, he was so very angry. So very angry, and he never gets angry like that. I remember the anguished sound he made, and I never want to hear that again.

I remember ringing our daughter in America. Rochelle, how do I tell you your brother is gone when you are so far away? And how do I hug you?

I remember calling my brothers and sister – how do I tell them their nephew is gone?

I remember his friends who had come to the flat to visit him only to find ambulance, police, people, but no Craig, because he was gone.

I remember saying goodbye to Craig in the ambulance – no, don't close the door, don't go. I want my son.

Time blurs – I remember a doctor – we are back home, and mum has called a doctor to check on me. I am fine; am I really fine? No, I am functioning, just. I fall asleep, and that day is etched in my memory.

A new day dawns, life has changed, and it will never, ever be the same. The next week blurs, there is so much to do, so many forms to fill out and a funeral to be arranged. I have to arrange for Rochelle and her husband to fly over here in time for the funeral. It is set for 10<sup>th</sup> of October. There are so many people to tell.

I remember the funeral, and so many, many people attended. Craig had so many friends. Why? is the question on everyone's lips. He was the least likely to commit suicide. There was no indication. No answer. I did the eulogy, which was so very hard. Peter spoke, Rochelle spoke. There were so many beautiful words.

I remember after the funeral speaking with his friends – please do not forget Craig. The years will come, your lives will go on – please do not forget him. In some corner of your life, remember there was a person called Craig. He lived 23 years, left no children, only memories. Please hold those memories. This is a fear of mine that he will be forgotten. I remembered, then, that his name would be forever inscribed on the shield at Bald Hills Primary School as Dux of his school. A small thing, perhaps, but an important legacy.

Suicide – it is a word only a word they say, but oh what a word that has so many, many emotions linked to it. It is a word that scares people, and they don't know what to say to you. It is a word that causes ripples that effect so many people.

It could have been so easy for Craig's suicide (there, I have said the word) to have broken our marriage. It did not. I remember Peter and I sitting down, holding each other, vowing that we would get through this together, that we would remember Craig, and we would live each day for Craig. We are still together, 43 years married. We visit Craig nearly every week, taking flowers. We speak about him, and he is here with us.

It was the months after, when I was processing everything, that I sat and thought about how Craig's suicide has impacted things. It came to me that there is a group who don't have anyone to speak with, a group who are hit twice as hard – and they are my parents, and Peter's parents. Not only have they lost a grandson, but they had to see their children go through an agonising situation that they could not help them with. Who do the grandparents speak to?

My brothers and sister lost a nephew, and their children lost a cousin. Rochelle lost a brother – her only brother – one she had not seen for many years. The tragedy was that he was booked to fly over to see her at Christmas.

Then there were his many friends who were left asking themselves, why? Why did they not see that there was something wrong? How could they not have seen and helped? There was nothing *to* see.

Our family goes on, and the impact is that the Springsteen name will not go on. Craig was to be the one to have the children, to carry the name on, to have our grandchildren. Rochelle can't have children. There will be no grandchildren for Peter and I, and that is hard to live with at times. Christmas and family gatherings can be hard when I see my sister and my brother becoming grandparents.

It is thirteen years this year. There have been many tears over those years. If my car could talk, it would tell of the many times driving back and forth to work when I have cried and cried. There is a hole in my heart that will never heal. Time blurs. Life does go on.

I have people say it is been so many years, why are you still crying? You should have healed. Well, no, people, you do not heal from this. You learn to live, you learn to laugh, and you learn to love. You grieve, you get up, but you do not heal. It is okay to cry – tears cleanse the soul – when I cry, I am remembering him.

Speak about those you have lost. For such a long time, suicide has been taboo, and you never mentioned those who had gone. Don't wipe out the time they have been with you. Honour the good memories and remember them.

Find support. There are many groups; some you will resonate with and others you will not. The best I have found are those who have travelled the journey that you have. They know what it is like because they have been there, and they can relate.

I remember Craig. I remember our son. I remember the sweet times, the funny times, the joyful times and the birthdays. I remember the day he chose to leave. I remember the sadness and the bitter. I remember you.

My life goes on with a hole in my heart, and the never answered question of Why? remains. I remember. Never, never forgotten.

## CRAIG ALLAN SPRINGSTEEN (ETCHI)

### 13 JULY 1984 TO 3 OCTOBER 2007

His spirit is free, and he lives in our heart for always.

Friend, please don't mourn for me

I'm still here, though you don't see.

I'm right by your side each night and day

and within your heart I long to stay.

My body is gone but I'm always near.

I'm everything you feel, see or hear.

My spirit is free, but I'll never depart

as long as you keep me alive in your heart.

*(Excerpt from "I'm Still Here" – Author Unknown)*

This chapter is from the soon to be published book *Remembering Craig – His Story.*

*If you wish to connect with Trish, you can contact her via her email: trish@trishspringsteen.com*

# In the Presence of Death

Michelle Fay Minchin

He was seated in his shiny new blue car, just sitting in the driver's seat, a can of alcohol in the console. I didn't recognise the brand, but I knew it was alcohol. He looked as if he was asleep. I knew he wasn't, because the blotchy purple and grey tinge to his skin assured me that he was dead, and he had been dead a while. His lips were purple from carbon monoxide poisoning – a deliberate intent on his part to take his own life.

I knew then that we were spiritual beings having a human experience on this planet, and yet the prevailing feeling of sadness I felt in the air was overwhelming, almost suffocating.

The fact that his mother was wailing in her grief undoubtedly added to this ominous feeling. He was only 20 years into his journey on this earth. What could have gone so horribly wrong for him to want to end his life so abruptly? This question pounded in my head. Why?

His mother sat howling in her sorrow, spraying grief over the yard and encompassing her remaining children who stood close by, immobile, just staring at her. The grief showed on their ashen faces and their downcast eyes and crestfallen shoulders. This was a family in mourning, and they had just lost one of their own.

I had to take charge of the situation. I was, after all a Police Officer, and it was my job to bring order to the situation. I called to the children to move inside and have a cup of tea (keep them occupied). I stated that their mother would join them soon. No one moved. I belted out a command and they dispersed uneasily, wary of me and keeping their eyes on me, protective of their mother. They shuffled away into the house and away from the scene.

I crouched down to see into the mother's eyes. This grief-stricken woman was still howling uncontrollably, and the sound was awful and almost electrifying in its intensity. Her sobs visibly shaking her body as she gulped for air. I took hold of her trembling right hand and said loudly, "Stop!". I don't know whether it was my touch she felt or the words she heard me speak, but she stopped abruptly and looked into my eyes.

Her eyes were wild, searching mine, looking for answers. She spoke in a soft whimper, "My son, my son." This was a delicate situation where a woman's religion and its dogma of beliefs were twisting her mind, and her thoughts were raging. The Christian religion teaches that suicide is sinful and an act of blasphemy, and yet her son had been a loving, Christian boy.

I could see the conflict and confusion in her face, which contorted with the myriad of thoughts rolling through her mind relentlessly. I spoke softly to this sobbing woman, "I want you to take a deep breath with me, o.k.?" She nodded in comprehension, and as she did the fresh tears under her eye lids rolled down her cheeks dripping onto her wrinkled brown linen dress, leaving visible wet patches.

"Take a deep breath in through your nose." We breathed deeply in unison. "Now breathe out through your mouth, slowly." This helped the woman to change her focus. She followed my instructions as I continued to breathe in and out with her. The body-shaking sobs subsided, and the tears stopped, leaving the poor lady looking rather like a large, crumpled rag doll.

I explained to this woman that her husband would be here soon, that we had called him, and he was on his way, and she could take as long as she needed to gather herself together. I explained to her that her remaining children needed her, that she is the backbone of the family and that they looked to her for support and guidance.

She nodded her understanding of my words. I then asked her if she wanted time alone – to gather her thoughts while I went inside to speak with the others. I waited for her reply. I could see she was trying to find the words in her confused mind. In the end she just nodded. As I stood up, I stated quietly, "I'm so sorry for your loss." I didn't know what else to say – what else could be said?

My thoughts would often return to this situation where religion and suicide had collided, where beliefs had been formed and then questioned, then shattered into tiny pieces. I, too, had been raised as a Christian, and had many years of doubt and disbelief. I believe the impact on me was strong because the woman was my age and her son was my son's age, and there by the grace of God, go I. Or so I believed.

Many years later, I was to find out exactly what this poor woman had felt – the gut-wrenching, nauseous pit-in-the-stomach feeling. An early morning phone call from my son pierced the morning air, and as I answered the phone, I had a sense something was wrong – a mother's intuition – or just that it was 4:00am in the blessed morning and that's a sure sign something's up.

My son stated he was just leaving the hospital and he wanted me to know he was o.k., that he had been revived and he was o.k.

My mind whirled with the fog of early morning wake-up. REVIVED! "What do you mean?" I asked urgently. He went on to say he had hung himself and that he had been found in time and they had revived him from his suicide attempt.

Hung himself – suicide – I heard the words. I was just trying to piece them together and make sense of them. Who would have thought all these years later, I would have to face the same questions of why regarding my son and his mental anguish? How could he have fallen so low that he felt the need to take his own life? Why didn't I see the signs?

I am highly trained in this. I have knowledge and experience with suicide. I knew my son was unhappy. I knew he felt trapped in a chaotic relationship, but I trusted he would figure it out. I didn't want to interfere in his life. I didn't want to give him the impression that I thought he couldn't make good decisions or that he couldn't cope.

How wrong I was. It's a fine line between helping your child and interfering in their lives. My son is a high functioning Autistic with unpredictable emotions. His situation became too hard, so his way of coping was to leave and to take his own life.

I was able to get him into emergency rehabilitation. I am forever grateful he was found in time and revived, and even though he isn't speaking to me at the moment, I'm glad he is still on his journey of life, still learning and still finding his way.


*If you wish to connect with Michelle, you can contact her via her email: shellsenergyhealing@yahoo.com*

# The Loss of a Sibling

Terri Tonkin

Have you ever felt like you have been kicked in the guts, and the wind taken right out of you? You are left speechless. You can't breathe. You can't move.

That's what it was like for me. I remember that feeling as if it was yesterday.

It was late on a Sunday night, the 3$^{rd}$ of October 1993. A day forever etched in my memory. The day my life, and my family's lives, changed forever. It seems so long ago, and yet it is still fresh in my mind. A day I will never forget.

My family, my husband and two boys, were living in Newcastle. My parents had come down from Brisbane, as my dad loved to see my son dance. He was very proud of all his children and grandchildren. After visiting with us, my parents were going to go to Wollongong to visit my brother.

On the Friday, we had travelled to Sydney for a ballroom dancing competition where my elder son was to compete in a two-day competition. We were fortunate that we were staying with a friend for the weekend.

My son enjoyed his dancing, and he won a few ribbons and medals throughout the competition. We all had a great weekend, watching the competition and catching up with friends.

We got home to Newcastle late on the Sunday night. We had not long got the car unpacked, and our neighbours came across to inform us the local police had been around, and they wanted us to contact them as soon as possible. Of course, this in and of itself was frightening. We all immediately assumed something had happened to my elder brother, who was working offshore in Vietnam on an oil rig. Our brains automatically went to the conclusion there had been and accident on the oil rig, and he was injured or worse.

My husband contacted the police station and they advised they would call around to see us. We were all on edge, not knowing what had happened. Within 15 minutes, the police arrived. Both my dad and husband went outside to talk with them. It seemed like time stopped, and we were in limbo.

When they came inside, my husband hugged me and our children. Dad knelt down beside mum, held her hand, and delivered the shocking news. My mum let out an ear-piercing scream. I can still hear it clearly to this day, almost 27 years on.

In that moment, our lives changed forever.

My other brother in Wollongong had taken his own life. We only had scant details; however, we knew he had given himself a lethal injection. My brother was a nurse, a theatre nurse, at two local hospitals, and he had access to a range of drugs and medications. Apparently, he had mixed a lethal concoction, filled two syringes, inserted one in each arm and injected one; the second not required.

He was a fantastic nurse, compassionate and empathetic, so to hear he had used his position to arrange his own demise was heartbreaking and very hard to understand, for his family and his work colleagues.

Trying to comprehend the situation was surreal. How could this have happened? Why didn't we know he was so unhappy? What had occurred for him to believe this was the only way out? What about his family? Did anyone know he was planning this? His work colleagues? So many questions, so few answers.

We started to contact my older brother and our extended family and friends. None of us were thinking clearly. I had to take the phone from dad a number of times, as he was unable to speak.

My dad contacted the local police where my brother was found. We got some more details. He had been found early on that Sunday morning, in his car, with his belongings (more questions), on a patch overlooking the beach. It was a beautiful stretch of coastline, so peaceful.

Friends and family arrived from Brisbane. Our house was full, which was a good thing. We all had someone to talk to. My boys, aged 12 and 9 at the time, were amazing. They were so attentive to my mum and dad, not letting them be by themselves at any time. We made our plans to pick up my brother flying in from Vietnam, and worked out how we would get everyone to Wollongong and arrange accommodation.

My dad visited the police station and was provided with a copy of a letter my brother had written. My brother was so devastated about the breakdown of his family; he felt he couldn't go on without his children in his life. We knew things were not good, but no-one had any idea of the extent. My dad had spoken to him on the Thursday, and even commented they would see each other on Tuesday. Tuesday would have been my brother's birthday. He would have celebrated his 38th year on earth.

At the funeral, the tension between the families was very intense. And this was only the beginning of the end. I know I was very angry with my brother. How dare he do this, knowing that I would have mum and dad with me? How dare he put me in this position? How could he do this to me? This was so unfair. Leaving me to be the one to hold everyone together.

I found hot showers to be my best friend. I managed to have quite a lot. If I was emotional, that is where I would go. I was trying to keep things together for mum, dad and my family. You see, dad had been battling cancer for 3 years when this happened, and that was pressure enough for him and mum. He had been putting up a good fight and was positive he would beat it. On this day, he gave up his fight. This had sucked the fight and life out of him. My anger levels were heightened. Of course, there was also sadness, grief, disbelief, and guilt. What a mixture of emotions going on, all at the same time. You can understand why a hot shower was a good friend.

My elder brother was a boiling pot of emotions. He was angry, he blamed others, he was hurt, he was frustrated. And he lashed out at my brother's family, in particular his wife, our sister-in-law. He blamed her and let her know it. Today, all these years later, he still holds anger and blame in his heart.

Not only did my nephew and niece lose their father, but they also lost our side of the family. We tried to maintain contact; however, it was rejected. Birthday cards went unacknowledged. Christmas presents were left at the house; I never knew if they were accepted. For almost 20 years, there was no contact.

It was only when my younger son located his cousin on Facebook, that we reconnected. He now has a son, a grandson my brother will never know. To this day, I have had no contact with my niece, who also has children, two girls. My nephew and niece have grown up not knowing their cousins and their children. This is very sad, for all of them, and for me. My brother loved being a family man, and loved his children dearly.

My parents lost a son. I lost a brother. My children lost an uncle. And the same for my other brother. His friends lost a good mate. His colleagues lost a valued nurse.

It was not only the family feeling the effects of his passing.

As I said previously, he was a nurse at two local hospitals. He was so highly thought of by the staff at one hospital that a colleague of his prepared and delivered the eulogy at his funeral. It was so moving, so poignant, it brought everyone to tears. He was much loved. The hospital held a memorial for him, and had a plaque mounted in the hospital chapel in his honour. All of his colleagues spoke highly of him. They said he was such a great theatre nurse, as he would sit with patients and make sure they were not frightened before procedures, and would be there when they woke up to reassure them all had gone well. It didn't matter if it was a young child or an elderly person, he was the one there holding their hand.

After a period of time after his passing, I began to understand why he had done what he did, and when he did it. The exact reason I was angry was important to the timing of the act. He loved his children; they were his world. He believed with the family breakdown that he wouldn't be allowed to be the father he wanted to be for them. And he couldn't live with that. The timing, he knew mum and dad would be taken care of, as they were with me, and surrounded by family.

My brother had his reasons for doing what he did, and when he did it. There were many things that had happened in his life that we were not aware of. He had put on a brave face for many years, it appears. His colleagues had noticed changes, yet he passed it off as an off day. No one really knew what was happening, or to what extent.

He had maintained contact with mum and dad on a regular basis. It wasn't as often with me, yet we still talked. We hadn't lived in the same location since I had left home at the age of 18. I had moved to Melbourne with the Defence Forces, married, and moved around with my husband. We visited from Melbourne, Ipswich, Darwin and Wagga Wagga. Geographically, we definitely were not close.

I went through the what ifs, if onlys, and many other scenarios. I will never know if I could have been able to change his mind, make him reconsider his choices, or helped him work out a compromise so that he would still be an active father in his children's lives. These questions will never be answered.

My brother's situation led me to the path of personal development, understanding why we do things, how we respond/react, how to interact with others, to have compassion and empathy, and how to work with others to support them through times such as these.

I can only hope and trust that if a friend or family member is ever in this situation, they will reach out and let people know they are not coping as well as they wish to. They may be considering similar actions. I like to believe I would be able to assist them to find an alternative action.

If you know anyone that is not their usual self, reach out to them, check in on them, ask if they are okay, what is it they need, or how can you assist.

If you have lost a friend or family member to suicide, please reach out also. You, too, deserve to have care provided to you, to work through the circumstances and go through the grief process. And please remember, everyone grieves differently. Do not let anyone tell you time will heal, it's time to move on. You will grieve the way you need to, in your own time.

For me, I found talking about what happened, how it impacted us all, and continuing to talk about my brother and his crazy antics has helped me to move through the process.

Sadly, suicide is still a taboo subject in many cultures and homes. No-one can understand what that person was going through, what emotions were filling their body, or even contemplate the dire position they had found themselves in. Let's lift the shame, blame and guilt around this.

And this goes for those left behind. The impact on them can also include shame, blame and guilt. When someone is contemplating suicide, and they make the decision to follow through, research suggests they have a plan of where, when and how. They have made up their minds.

This is my belief. For those of us impacted, we need to believe our loved one had decided there was no alternative. They chose to be responsible for their decision. Send them love, remember them with love, talk about them with love. You may never understand the reasons, and they are not your reasons to understand. I have my thoughts around my brother's reasons, yet I will never know if they are correct. Remember them for the wonderful person they were, and the way they made you feel when you were around them.

My brother is still my brother, he is still my parents' son, he is still my children's uncle.

Rest In Peace.

*If you wish to connect with Terri, you can contact her via her email: terri@connectwithin.com.au*

# Suicide – The Only Option!

Paula Burgess

When one reaches the age of 20 and is no longer a teenager, their whole life is ahead of them. A "real" adult, beyond the teenage years.

Not for me, though. I could see nothing ahead of me, and according to my brain, I was worthless, and felt I had not achieved anything in life, nor was I really working towards anything.

As a young child, I felt I was never good enough, and my sister was always the better person. You see, my dad was both physically and mentally abusive, but funnily enough, he only took his frustration out on my mother and I, and left my sister alone.

I distinctly remember at the age of 10 that I needed my first set of glasses (which I should have had years before), and my dad had it in his head that the optometrist was just ripping mum off. As a child, I still remember dad yelling at mum so much that I cowered in the hallway believing that this was my fault because I needed glasses.

Then, something even worse happened! Dad threw my mother's head into a brick wall! This was my fault!

As a 10-year-old little girl, my mother was my world, and to think that something I needed was the cause of her being hurt was a huge burden.

Apparently, dad then turned his anger to the optometrist, but I ended up with my glasses in the end.

Of course, that wasn't the end of my run-ins and abuse, and as I got older, I remember being the recipient of a great deal of it.

Finally, when I was 14, my mother had the courage to leave my father, and I was elated but my sister was devasted! That just proved to me the difference in treatment that we received as siblings.

However, my father was not going away quietly. There were times he turned up to the house, yelling at everyone. Sometimes he was drunk, and he would come over and threaten all of us. One night, I remember him being in our house and he threw my cat and my 3-legged dog down the stairs.

I'd had enough, and I lost it and screamed at my father. My animals were the last straw for me, so I grabbed them and my little sister, and we hid in her room away from him, and mum threatened to call the police. I think this was the very first time my sister understood why mum was leaving!

Not long after that, mum announced we were definitely leaving our home! We were moving from Rockhampton down to Brisbane, away from our friends and mum's family AND my favourite cousins!

Although I didn't really want to move, I knew we had to get away from Dad. Then, the unthinkable happened! Dad asked me to stay and live with him! Wow! Like that was going to happen!

However, the real reason that he wanted me to live with him was because he wanted my sister to live with him, and she wouldn't stay if I didn't agree to stay. He didn't really want me after all, he just wanted my sister!

Although I was happy to get away from dad, I was not happy to be moving away from my friends and family. There was nothing I could do though, as it was decided.

At 14 years of age, the damage to my self-worth was done. I was already overweight and an average (and even borderline failing) student. This was the 11th school I had been to, so I found it difficult to make friends. The rift was evident between my sister and I, and we didn't really get along that well.

My mother met another man who treated us well, and eventually things settled down and were starting to get back on a positive track.

Then dad came to visit us and took my sister and I out to dinner. At the time, the song "Janie's got a gun" was popular and it happened to come on the radio while dad was driving us home. Much to my surprise he started singing "Daddy's got a gun" and then proceeded to tell me that he had a gun that he could use anytime.

This scared the life out of both my sister, and I and as soon as we got home, we told mum we didn't want to see him again.

A year or two later, my father had moved to Melbourne and my sister wanted to visit him, but mum wouldn't let her go without me, so I had to go.

Dad came and collected us and took us down to the Gold Coast for a "fun" holiday, and his brother and sister-in-law were joining us. This made it better, as I really loved my Aunt and Uncle.

After a few days together things were going ok, until I decided not to do an activity dad wanted to do. I told dad that, he and my sister could do it and I would just wait.

However, he wasn't having a bar of this, and insisted I do it with him, but I didn't want to. He promptly slapped me across the face and told me that I asked for that as I looked like my mother, something I wasn't able to help of course.

I just wanted to go home after that, but of course that wasn't going to happen. My father monitored every phone call I made to my mother from then on, to be sure I didn't tell her. However, I did tell my Auntie, and she managed to get word to my mother about it and mum was worried.

Then dad took us to Melbourne, and a few more things happened but nothing I can remember clearly. However, I do remember when we were close to my stepfather's mother's house that mum called the police to see what could be done about getting us back if she needed to, and told me to go to my step-grandmother's house if needed and the police would be notified.

I didn't get the opportunity to do this to get away from dad, but we did get home safely, and for years after that I refused to see my father again.

Being failed so badly by the main male role model in my life had a huge impact on my self-esteem.

I was then old enough to have a serious boyfriend, and he was lovely; he had had a pretty bad upbringing as well, so he got me. That didn't stop me from pushing him into situations where he would want to hit me, after all that is what I was used to, right? He never did though, thankfully.

We then started to grow apart and want different things, so we broke up. Although this was a mutual decision, it was still a hard one. We had been together for quite a few years and had even talked about marriage.

Like any breakup, it takes a toll on your self-worth.

I then met another man who was 15 years my senior and already had 3 children! No matter how much pursuing I did, he was pushing me away as he did not feel we were suited given his already lived life. Suddenly, my life was spiralling again!

To top off everything going on in my life, my stepfather gave me a letter to tell me he loved me (not as a daughter, either)! How on earth was I going to tell my mother! It was just another blow that I had to deal with from a trusted male in my life!

My self-confidence was terrible, and I had no one to talk to! I didn't feel I would amount to anything; I had no career projection, I had broken up with my first love, I didn't feel my father loved me, my stepfather had hit on me, and a man I really liked didn't want me, and on top of this he told me he had slept with someone else!

We hadn't discussed being exclusive, but in my mind we were. So, it hurt... a lot!

Then, one night, I was at his place and he was out, and I made the decision that I didn't want to be here any longer and that no-one would really miss me if I was not here anymore. I took a handful of pills in the hope that I would just fall asleep and never wake up.

However, I was found. It was too early for me at the time, but now I look back and I am thankful that I was found. I was rushed to hospital and promptly taken care of.

I remember one particular nurse as she was giving me charcoal to soak up the tablets, chastising me and telling me how I was wasting their time with what I had done, and they could be caring for people who needed it.

Certainly not something that someone with self-worth issues wants to hear, it just made me feel worse! I was moved up to the ward and watched closely for the next few days.

Unbeknownst to me, my mother had called my father and he raced to the hospital the next day. This was a turning point of my life! When my father walked to my hospital bed, I saw a totally different man! I saw someone who was broken, someone who couldn't understand why his daughter would do this, someone who was about to fall to pieces.

Over 25 years later, I still remember the look on his face! His face at the time told me that he really did love me, and this was something that I had never really believed.

I spent some time in therapy sorting myself out and started to get my life back on track.

Fast forward, many years, I am now married to that man who is 15 years older than me, and we have a child together. I have achieved so much in my life, and I realise that so many other people's lives would have been impacted with my passing.

I have since rebuilt the relationship with my father, and mum and dad are back together after 20 years apart. We all live together at the same address (different houses though)! Now that I understand the mindset that my father had at the time, it has helped me understand his view on life. He must live with the consequences of his actions, not me. I have done the personal work that I needed to do to get through this.

I revisited this headspace once again a few years ago, but I can honestly say it scared me! I identified the signs and made the conscious choice to do a lot of work through personal development, talking to people and meditation to get me through it.

I can see now that there are many reasons why I survived this, and I am thankful to be here every day. One particular reason is my son. I know I was meant to be here to ensure that he is here. He is changing the way people see things with the way he is, and I am sure he will do things that I can't even conceive of right now. He has changed my perspective on life, and he challenges everyone in his path with his out-of-the-box thinking.

I look at my son now and I am confident that we have an open and supportive relationship. He trusts me enough to talk to about anything. I hope that as he moves into those precious teenage years that the lines of communication can remain open and our talks continue, so he never has to feel like he has no one to turn to.

If you are a parent reading this and you wonder how you can support your child (or a friend) so that they don't get to this stage, here are my tips from my perspective:

- Communication – continually check in with your children and be interested in what is happening in their life. Ask questions and get the answers. Do not accept "I don't know" or "not much" as answers; change your questioning to encourage them to answer.
- Get interested – like I said before, ask questions. Let your child know that you are interested in their life and what they are doing, and be present when they are talking to you. Put down the phone or computer and listen to what they have to say. It may bore the pants off of you, but do it anyway. You are showing you them you are an open book of communication and they will talk to you.
- Be a safe person – be that person they can bring anything to. Be supportive of them. If they have done something wrong, try not to rant and rave about it (I know this can't be helped sometimes), but talk it out instead. Help them understand that it is safe to be honest with you. Better that than having them feel like they have to lie or cover things up. Kids will be kids, and they will hide things from you, but if you are safe, they are less likely to hide

things and they will come to you with a problem. If you can't be that safe person then talk to them about identifying someone who can be.

- Be aware – use you parent instinct! If you think something is wrong, it probably is! Be prepared to ask the hard questions. If you feel they are depressed and are heading down that road to suicide, ask the question and monitor as much as possible. If there is one thing I know, it's that when you are in that headspace, there is nothing anyone can say to get you out of it. But if I'd had a trusted person before I got there, then maybe it wouldn't have come to that point.

- Get help – don't do this alone! If you are worried about anyone who may be depressed or might turn to suicide for an answer, get help! There are so many more support options out there today than there was in my time, so just find them. Even by just calling places like Lifeline or Kids Help Line or even your child's school if they are still at school, then they can all direct you to the places where you can get the support you need.

I hope my story helps you to have a better understanding of the mindset of someone who does this. Obviously, every story is different, but this is my story. I understand what it is like to be in this space where I felt no-one could have helped me, however, if I had access to some of the support from the tips I shared above, I may not have ended up there in the first place. But maybe I needed to go through what I went through in order to achieve what I have achieved. Who knows what my life path will bring!

*If you wish to connect with Paula, you can contact her via her website: www.beyondthemaze.com.au*

# Why, Why, Why???

Rita-Marie Lenton

*A Funeral Director's Perspective*

This is a question that rips at the very heart of everyone with a close family member that has taken their own life.

With the question comes the guilt: why didn't I see this coming? I should not have let them go home alone! Why didn't I stay with them? On and on, the thoughts rush around in your mind.

This is what tears at the core of every family member and friend. Having experienced suicide in my own family more than once I, too, struggle with these questions. I have seen first-hand the disbelief, the anger, the guilt and the utter devastation that is left behind. It is through these experiences that I am able to understand and help families say farewell to their loved ones.

In my twenty years in the funeral industry, I have looked after several families going through the motion of arranging a funeral. My first experience with arranging a funeral for someone who had passed through suicide was for a young man. The thing that got me was his dog. The family spoke about how his dog was found at the scene; he hadn't left his master. They explained that the dog was grieving, and they wanted permission to have his dog come to the funeral. Of course, the answer was yes. When they arrive for the viewing they asked if they could bring the dog into the room. I still feel chills as I stood outside the door of the viewing room listening to the cries of that dog, his grief at the loss of his master was just as real as the family's. This was my first funeral relating to suicide outside of my own family, and possibly one of the hardest. During the service, the dog sat with coffin, and the family had to pick him up and carry him from the chapel when the time came for them to leave.

The next time suicide touched me closely was receiving word that one of our own, Trish Springsteen, had lost her son Craig to suicide. I knew who Trish was – she was the one-time manager of the crematorium where I started my career, I had met her one or twice. Trish arranged the service via our branch manager in Redcliffe, then as the after-hours arranger it was my job to look after the viewing for Craig's friends, which the family organised for them the night before the service.

My job that night was to set Craig up in the chapel and be on hand while the friends come to say their private farewell to Craig. What was to be an hour viewing turned into three hours. As Trish and her family had a private family viewing earlier in the day, I met with her husband Peter and her sister Jacquie as they were on hand to greet Craig's friends. When Craig's friends arrived, for the first 30 minutes they mainly sat outside of the chapel speaking in hushed tones, berating themselves for not picking up on the struggles Craig had. Gradually, they came one by one and paid their respects. The comments I heard each time was how sorry they were that they had let Craig down.

I felt honoured to be able to help Trish's family and friends through this time. The hardest part of the night for me was letting them know it was time for them to leave. Over the years, Trish and I have become close friends. We share a common bond, as I am now the manager of the crematorium where Trish served all those years ago, and it is now Craig's forever home.

Over my twenty years, there have been many families I have met because of suicide. I have guided them through the process of the funeral arrangements and viewing their loved one. This is where my thinking cap is placed squarely on my head, as I advise them on the type of clothing to provide. Sometimes, it is not possible for a viewing due to the length of time before they were found. In this case, I have always suggested private time with the closed coffin, suggesting that they write a letter to their loved one that they can place on the coffin. Another popular way of saying goodbye is to allow friends and family to write their messages directly onto the coffin. It is especially important to ask the family to bring the kind of music their loved one listened to.

A funeral service is important for both the family and the friends, so that they have time to grieve to share their stories, and most importantly, where possible, share the life of their loved one in pictures.

While statistics say young men have the highest suicide rate, I have learned that both women and men take their own lives, from all ages and many walks of life. We don't always know the answer to "why". I have learned not to judge because, for the deceased, they feel the world is a far better place without them here.

For the ones left behind, a piece of my heart goes with them as we all continue to question how we could have stopped it, and the guilt because we couldn't stop it. This is then followed by our need to blame someone for what has happened.

I know in my heart, from my own family members, that there was nothing we could have done to stop the outcome. From the clairsentience side of me, I know they are sorry for the pain they left behind, and I would like to think they are all now at peace.

# War of the Kevins
## Kevin Hill

When I was a young teen, I would go to my friend's house. We closed the door, switched off the light and would play one of my favourite albums. The only light emitted was the blue light from the fish tank as we played "Jeff Wayne's – War of the Worlds". Jeff had taken the story from H. G. Wells and made it into a musical. The fusion of the eerie blue light and the soundtrack was an amazing experience. Little did I know just much this album would influence my life! More of how this album affected my whole life and suicide attempt later.

Today, I am a resilience expert and a life coach. I am also the UK's number #1 suicide intervention coach. I have spoken and coached across the globe. I speak, coach and train people of all ages. I have programs for adults, teens and children. I have confidence, and I know who I am and what my purpose is for my life.

However, if you come back with me to when I was a teenager, it was a very different story. On one side, I was very powerful and actively going after my goal. I was totally immersed in martial arts. It was my whole life. I lived and breathed for the martial arts. My club allowed me to do Karate, Judo, Aikido and Tai Chi. I was progressing through the training and the belts at quite a rapid rate. Due to my involvement, it also meant that I had power to do a lot of things. I took up the martial arts in order to fight back the bullies.

On the flip side, I was a mess. I was a scrambled egg of a person. Even as a teenager, I had years of depression weighing down on me. The ever-growing rejection oozed out of every pore. Paradoxically, loneliness was my best and only friend. Constantly being bullied at school and on my street. Whoever had said that "childhood are the best years of your life" had not lived at my house.

My life was one of two halves, but neither the "Power Life" nor the "Broken Life" were the real me. I was the very small and insignificant person in the middle, desperate to be seen and known. Nobody ever noticed the real Kevin Hill, as they only saw one side of me. Everyone saw either the powerful guy who liked to make jokes to mask his pain, or an easy target for bullying. No-one saw the brokenness of living with the heavy, relentless taskmasters of depression, rejection and loneliness. A civil war was taking place in my head, and it was not pretty at all.

The dark storm clouds of depression crashed into my life when I was only five years old. I do not have any memories from before I was five, but I do remember one day, when I was five, in particular. I was sat on the windowsill looking down the long drive to the air base. My father was in the air force. Someone called my name. I turned round to see who it was and what they wanted. It was time to eat dinner. It was fish fingers, chips and peas. In the room was my twin brother, my sister, my older brother and someone else. My parents were not there. This was the day my father died.

Enduring bullying throughout my childhood and school days was extremely difficult. What made it worse was the bullies lived on my street, so I would get bullied at school and on my street. It was every time they saw me, as there was always a group of bullies, and they made my life miserable. The "Aliens" – the false Kevins had invaded, and began to attack. The War of the Worlds was becoming a daily reality for me.

From the age of about ten onwards I would often walk by myself, thinking of ways I could kill myself. Just like the "Red Weed" from

"War of the Worlds", these lies had crept into my mind and was poisoning it from the inside. The red weed stuck and grew incessantly in my head. Yes, even at that early age, I wanted to die. I would go through different scenarios weighing the pros and cons of each situation. I would think about stuff like how quick or how painful each way to die would be. The red weed lies began as a whisper, but grew louder and louder until they screamed at me most days. The red weed lies taunted me with stuff like:

"You are not loved by anyone."

"You are useless!"

"No one will miss you when you are gone."

"You are worthless and will never amount to anything."

These lies became a driving force within me. There was no escape from their voices, and fuelled by the rejection and the depression, things were about to take a nasty turn.

A few years later, when I was at the tender age of sixteen, I reached the point in the civil war that finally broke me. The point in War of the Worlds where the humans had lost all hope. I, too, was about to lose all hope. I was never good at getting up in the mornings. This one day I was late for work. I had left school and worked in an ice cream factory. I rushed off to work, shooting a quick "Morning" to my mum who was in the chair. An hour or so later, two police came to my work asking to talk to me. Then came the devastating blow.

"Sorry son, your mum died early this morning."

I was so late for work that I rushed out thinking mum was asleep in the chair, not even realising that she had died there. This was the last straw. The fragile world of Kevin came crashing down. It pushed me right to the edge. I felt as though I had lost everything and was completely alone now. At the time I had two brothers and a sister, but still felt completely empty and desperately alone.

My mum's death just served to empower the red weed lies and propel me closer to suicide. I had a friend who worked on lathes. He sharpened a lock knife I had. At the ice cream factory, we usually had our break time with at least one other person. However, this one particular day I was in on my own. I had been taking the knife to work for a while now. Taking it out, I played with the knife for a short time then raised it up above my head. I brought the knife down on my wrist. At the point where I just nicked my skin, the words of one of the songs from War of the Worlds came crashing into my mind like a run-away train.

"There must be something worth living for

There must be something worth trying for

Even some things worth dying for

And if one man can stand tall

There must be hope for us all."

I was frozen with those lyrics reverberating around my head and the knife poised on my wrist. All concept of time disappeared. At some point, those words entered into me and my thinking began to change.

"Maybe there was something worth living for?" I began to ponder. For the first time that I could remember, there was a glimmer of hope for me. That glimpse of hope was enough to keep me alive. I slowly folded the knife and slid it into my pocket, wiped and covered up my wrist, and went back to work. I didn't tell my work colleagues, nor my family and friends. No-one knew for many years what had happened.

I still wandered round in a lost daze for over a year. Many people find something that helps them; for me, it was finding out who I was and what my purpose was. For me, this all began to happen when I had an encounter with God. I became a Christian when I was seventeen. It radically changed my life. I became a "Child of God". The "War" was over, and I could begin to rebuild my life. My purpose was to help people, especially children and teens. That is a vision and goal I have been building on since that time.

From that time, Kevin the scrambled egg was put back together. It was a lot like the intro to a TV show.

"We can rebuild him. We have the technology. We can make him better than he was before. Better, stronger, faster."

- Spoken Intro from "The Bionic Man", a 1980's TV show

I was getting healed, and the red weed lies withered up until they had completely died out. Now, I was very happy that they had died out and not me. I was alive, *felt* alive, and looked forward to enjoying life.

Many years later I became a certified life coach, specialising in coaching children and teens. As part of that great work, I encountered children with many of the issues I had as a child or teen. They needed something more, so I studied resilience and how to build that into their lives. Then, someone asked if anyone knew of anyone who had survived a suicide attempt. Hey! That was me! I had survived, and now I could help other people with my story. I contacted them and shared my story. Two major realisations happened. One was that my story was powerful, and the second was that people need help in the area of suicide awareness and intervention. I went on suicide intervention courses and created a fusion of life coaching and suicide intervention to become a suicide

53

intervention coach. I called this service *"Grim Reaper Ain't a Keeper"* because the grim reaper didn't keep me, and is going to lose his grip on others who will live and not die by suicide. I had survived, and there was hope for others. They, too, could defeat the "Red Weed Lies" and the "Aliens" attacking them.

***Don't Check Out … Reach Out!***

*Contact Kevin Hill: Resilience & Life Coaching*

*GreatKidsLifeCoach@gmail.com*

*Suicide Intervention: grimreaperaintakeeper@gmail.com*

*Kevin Hill is R.E.E.L: – Resilience Expert in Education and Life. Kevin empowers people, especially children and teens, to build and maintain resilience into their lives. Kevin shows them how to bounce back and rediscover their Zing and Mojo. This is achieved through coaching, training and speaking. Kevin is also the UK's #1 suicide intervention coach.*

# It's A Boy
Rosalie Webb

"It's a boy." Four older sisters and at last, a son to carry on the family name. So wanted, so loved. Adored by all. It seemed that no child had been craved more than this one.

My father found that although he had a son, he had no time to spend with him, as the family trucking business took all his attention. It could be considered that part of this was a lack of desire to participate, and part of it was a shortage of time. My brother's cricket practice, football games, musical events and school functions were all either avoided or unattainable by my father. How to compensate; give him the best of everything, all the things his older sisters didn't have, send him to the best school; but that was not what my brother needed nor wanted.

Slowly, his life unravelled. His school results plummeted, peer pressure was strong; but was he a leader, or was he being led? It turns out it was both. He made bad decisions, associated with the wrong people, was introduced to drugs, found alcohol, but couldn't seem to uncover what he was really looking for.

How could this be happening to the handsome, intelligent boy he was?

He eventually gave up on school, and my parents could see that the private school fees were wasted on their son who was not in the least bit committed to study, a career or what the future may hold.

He worked hard, and always had a job, but they were not sustainable positions as employment, drugs, alcohol and depression are not compatible.

My brother knew how to work the system whereby he obtained unemployment benefits while endeavouring to have the majority of his employers pay him in cash; therefore, he enjoyed the best of both worlds. This extra money enabled him to continue to feed his drug and alcohol habit.

When my brother drank, he became aggressive, and this led to fighting, which inevitably headed towards trouble with the law. He became a heavy drinker at times, and drifted towards others who drank at the same level. It appears that he did manage to understand, even when he was heavily intoxicated, that one should not drink and drive, as he never lost his driver's licence nor had an accident, despite his heavy drinking sessions.

The drugs started out as mild usage, but escalated at times through his life as he needed them to disguise the demons that continued to infiltrate his mind and his every being.

My brother was 15 years younger than me. I left the small country town in Victoria where we resided not long after his birth. He called me Ro, no-one else but he could get away with shortening my name in such a way. All his sisters adored him and spoilt him, showering him with treats and gifts every time we saw him. Despite his shortcomings, as he got older, he was always well dressed and clean. He used an alluring aftershave that I can still smell to this day.

As we all went our way in life, the 5 siblings resided in different states of Australia. This meant we did not have regular contact unless it was by telephone. My brother had a fractured relationship with our youngest sister, which caused a lot of tension in the family.

She fought for the attention of my parents, and it appeared she went out of her way to show our brother in a bad light at every opportunity. This did not, by any means, help with all the monsters he was battling.

He appeared to be a drifter, a nomad; he tried to settle in one place, but the lure of something more important or extra exciting got in the way.

My brother moved from state to state seeking employment and a feeling of belonging. He came to live with me for a short period, and I was to discover that he was a genius when completing crosswords. And, if you expected you may win while playing him at Scrabble, think again. How could this sharp mind have such a loss of focus and purpose?

The one person who truly unconditionally loved him was my mother; she forgave him for all his indiscretions. She knew his faults, weaknesses and flaws, but that did not stop her from finding the good in him wherever possible. She did become frustrated with him at times, as shown in some of her diary entries where she wrote of his total lack of commitment to his responsibilities, including his many returns to home to live when life was out of control; the borrowing of money; his poor friendship choices; his aggressive nature when he wasn't sober; and his many problems including his dispiritedness and melancholy, but throughout all this, she continued to be his protector and pray daily that God would watch over him. She had a strong religious faith, and always believed God would look after her only son.

My brother was always looking for love, and many times it appeared he had found the love of his life. Most of the girls he formed relationships with were diamonds, but slowly his drinking and drug taking became too much, for even the most devoted woman. Parting was inevitable with depression and dejection taking over, each time becoming worse with every failed relationship. These relationships often brought a new life into the world, and there were many. He had a deep rapport with children, possibly because he never grew up himself. Every unsuccessful love affair was another lost child as well, and hence more misery followed.

There were very few things that my brother was truly attached to, but one of them was his 1972 Kingswood. It was Brunswick Green in colour and in immaculate condition; it truly was his prized possession. He went all over Australia in that car.

Father had a fractured relationship with his much-craved son. They both found it difficult, but both attempted to find an accord with each other. Father was a committed, reliable, conscientious man, whereas his son was the opposite. Father often felt let down. His son also felt abandoned by the man who was his father in name but mostly showed very little compassion. It appeared for most of his life the two had not bonded.

Mother died five years before her son. This was a true blessing, as it would have broken her heart to know he died so young.

After the death of my mother, my father slowly re-connected with my brother. They began to realise they did have things in common, one being that they were both hardworking, another that my brother had started to live a more orderly life. They both made an effort to mend their relationship, which was evident in discussions with my father after my brother had begun creeping more and more into our conversations. Truck driving seemed to be a good option for my brother in the latter years of his life, as this meant he would have to be drug and alcohol free. The problem with this preference was that the drugs and alcohol would mask the depression and mood swings, so they were not easy things to live without.

I received the call in the early hours of June 1st, 2008 from my father to tell me that finally, the black dog had caught my darling brother, and that he had passed away at his own hand.

My father had gone to visit him, as he did regularly, to talk about trucks, as now that my brother was a truck driver they both spoke the same language. These visits had become a regular occurrence in the last few years of his life. Every weekend, my father expected to get a call from my brother before visiting. One weekend, the awaited call did not come, so he went to my brother's house. On arrival, he asked a neighbour if he had seen my brother. The answer was negative, but he thought he could hear a humming noise coming from the house. I think my father knew straight away what he would find as he approached the house, and could hear the engine running of the treasured Kingswood in the garage.

My dear father. What an awful thing to discover; his beloved son had gone. He wanted to tell me every minute detail of his discovery; I didn't want to hear this, as I wept uncontrollably. I realised later it was a way of him trying to process what had happened.

There was so much I had not recognised. There always seemed to be a great detachment between us, whether in mind or in distance. If only I had lived closer and had possibly seen the signs; if only I had rung him more, if only I could have been a better sister. I had difficulty processing his death; because we lived in different states, I thought he would always be there. His death brought pain, confusion and self-recrimination. It is difficult to let go, to find healing and peace.

I have learnt that often we do not see or hear what is literally right there in front of us. It is so important to listen actively and to pay attention to what a person doesn't actually say in words. I need to be fully in the moment. For all his shortcomings, maybe everybody didn't respect what my brother was really trying to communicate. He was looking for unconditional love and happiness.

My brother, Warwick, was only 42 years, 3 weeks and 26 days old when life became too much.

*If you wish to connect with Rosalie, you can contact her via her email: rosalie.webb@bigpond.com*

# It's Not Over 'till it's Over

## Belinda Shaw

WHERE I WAS AT…

I sat in my red leather chair, knees up under my chin, rocking backwards and forwards and wishing I were dead.

I was wondering why my life was so revolting. I hated myself. I hated my life. I hated what it represented. I hated that I hadn't achieved the things that I thought I would have at that stage.

I lived in one of those terrible unit complexes that has security everywhere. You needed a key card to get through the front door, another to get you into your own unit. Once the door slammed behind you, you are on your own. I had often thought that if I died, no one would find me for weeks.

It's interesting what we can feel, and what we can take on from other people.

A couple of days prior, I had been yelled at by a guy I was dating: it was just this giant vomiting barrage of hateful, spiteful, nasty, vitriolic words that just flew out of his mouth all over me; things like "you let yourself go", "you've put on weight"; he was critical of the life coaching studies that I was doing, and suggesting that I didn't have what it took to run a business because he's been there and done that and he knew how hard it was and he knew that I didn't have it in me. There's no words of encouragement, no thoughts of "let's discuss it and see if there's anything I can offer to help you"; it was just a giant vomit of ugliness and spitefulness and hatred and "I don't care"s, and I just stood there and listened to the whole thing.

Why didn't I just turn around and run, I don't know; he had managed to wear me down to a point where I really thought that's all I was, I really thought my life had had turned to shit in a bucket so badly that I thought that was all I was worth.

That really was the straw that broke the camel's back. I went back to my unit. I just sat there, I couldn't move; I just felt sick, worthless, like my life did not matter one little bit. I had taken on board all the toxic things that this person had just spewed all over me as if it were mine and as if it was true, and all I deserved in my life was nothing.

At that point, I thought the only reasonable thing to do was to end it all. I sat in my chair realising what a fucking loser I was, that nobody would miss me. I was an oxygen thief. I was taking up space that somebody much better than me could be occupying. I didn't have a partner; I didn't have children. I had no-one to take care of me and no-one to take care of; no-one would miss me.

I had hit the shitty jackpot. I felt lonelier than I had ever felt in my whole life; I didn't know where I belonged, I didn't feel like I belonged anywhere. I certainly didn't feel smart enough, pretty enough, good enough. And I absolutely did not feel any love, not from anyone else and certainly not from me. I had no self-worth, zero self-esteem, I was at rock bottom. I wanted out.

I began planning what I would do as I was rocking back and forward in the chair. I thought I'd jump in my car go for a bit of a drive around. I knew there was a construction site up the highway, a new bridge was being built and I had worked out what angle I would have to do drive at the centre pylon in order to get the car at the right angle to kill myself. My car had all around air bags that would go off, so calculating that was interesting.

I've been married and divorced twice, both times I had been the one who left because I knew I was somehow worth more than what I was putting in or getting out of my marriages. I always see potential in people, always looking at life through rose coloured glasses, it's somehow prettier that way. And yet, I knew I was the common denominator of both of these relationships, and so I needed to do some work on me.

Why is it that the person who supposed to love you more than anything in the whole world, can't see that you have become desperately unhappy? And then it is a surprise when you leave. I just don't get that. I don't understand how you can be with somebody 24/7 and just not see that they're incredibly unhappy.

*Why would you not ask a question? Hey, how are you going? You seem to be a bit off colour today, is there anything wrong? Would you like to sit down and have a chat? Let's go for walk, let's go to the beach, let's do something. Let's just talk. Let's get out of our normal routine for five minutes. I can see that something is not quite right. Tell me what it is, I love you so much, I care for you more than anything, I can see that you're hurting, please tell me, please let me help you –* is all I wanted to hear from someone.

When I got stuck enough to want to take my own life, all I thought about is every single thing that went wrong, everything that I did, everything I didn't have, everything that made me feel like shit. I didn't just think about it once or twice, I went over and over and over until that's all that was left. Anything that was even remotely good was just piled into insignificance.

WHAT I DID NEXT...

There must've been some tiny shred of self-belief left, because I knew I wanted to tell somebody what I was about to do. I rang a friend in Melbourne – a lady I'd met at coaching school – and I told her everything that happened in the last few weeks that I was desperately unhappy.

The reason I'm still here today is that she said to me, "How do you think your mother would feel?" I hadn't given anybody outside of myself a second thought, except that I didn't think I would be missed.

That question that she asked me was the absolute turning point, because for that nanosecond I did think about my mum, and I suddenly realised that I couldn't do it to her; in that nanosecond it stopped being about me, and I thought about her, her life and the loss that she had already endured.

I knew then that I could never, and would never take my life in her living years; you can see that still gave me an out (which is no longer needed), but I just needed to make sure that I could get through now.

You see, mum had already experienced extreme loss in her life. My oldest brother, her firstborn child, died of cancer a number of years earlier, and she still grieves him. I don't believe that children should die before the parents, and the fact that she's already lost one ... I really didn't think I could make her go through that again. It must have been just enough to save me from hurting her anymore, so I decided to stay.

The journey back from that very ugly place has not been easy. It has been reflective, it has been filled with beautiful people, amazing conversations, heartfelt laughter, and a small tattoo inside my left wrist. I am the author; the story is my life, and it's not over yet.

The way I look at it, mum has given birth to me *twice*. She gave birth to me as baby, and she gave me life a few years ago, and for that I'll be forever grateful.

Some people may read this and think I'm a bit of a fraud because I didn't follow through; some people may read it and think about how courageous it was to reach out at the time. Some may wish that their loved ones had been given a nanosecond. I am truly, deeply sorry for your loss.

I went through the dark night of the soul, staring at that big black damn dog, and I truly believed that nobody would miss me if I wasn't here anymore, nobody would even blink sideways, no-one would go to my funeral.

WHERE I AM NOW...

I made a pact with my family. If I'm in a relationship with somebody who's saying all the right things to me, but horrible things to or about the people I love, that's not a nice person. I've made my family promise me that should I bring somebody home who is not nice, they must let me know what was done, said, or felt, so I can at least make an educated decision on continuing the relationship or not.

Someone said to me once – in fact, I've heard it a number of times – that the people who take their own lives are incredibly selfish, that they have a little regard for those who are left behind. But I have to tell you that when I was sitting in that chair, I really believed I would be doing the world a favour, I really didn't think that my life would count for anything.

I can't begin to express how incredibly grateful I am that I made that phone call. That I thought for that nanosecond about my mum, and that I'm still here.

Four words: Clarity, Strategy, Growth and Legacy. These are the cornerstones to all the work I do now. The framework for that is "Achieving Growth (spiritual, personal & professional) and Impact (another word for Legacy) through Clarity (clear thinking) and Strategy (we've got to have a plan and work the plan)".

The methods for delivery are Write, Travel & Speak.

I've written and published a book, *The Becoming of Wisdom – from Fragmented to Free*. It has already impacted lives in so far as it's giving people time to reflect upon their own journey, things that happened, situations they found themselves in, how they handled those situations, and how they can now let go. That gives me great joy.

Immediately prior to publication, I sat with mum to explain to her all of this, because it is part of the book and part of my life. She needed to hear it from me before someone mentioned it to her in conversation after they had read my book.

I had come home to live with her in our family home shortly after all of this had taken place, and after I had made some very poor financial decisions. I had hit rock bottom; mind, body, heart, spirit and finances completely shattered. My family home has given me a place to rest and recuperate and to find love once again – and that's not a love outside of me, it's a love of self, a love of life, and a love of the potentiality that life gives.

Travelling is something I wish to indulge in much more. There are so many incredible places to experience, and I plan to experience them all. In India last year, I stood in the Arabian Sea and decided that I wanted to put my feet in the sea of every land that I travel to. Strangely though, I understand that by paddling in the water at my local beach I am standing in water that has already kissed the shores of every land and every nation on this beautiful blue planet. All water flows to the sea. It is when I am near or in water that ideas flow, brilliance shines through, and the ebb and flow of life continues.

The speaking part is the stages on which I will present my philosophies on life, wisdom learned, and from which I will ask the hard questions to the people who are sick and dying, people who are oscillating, and perhaps those who don't wish to be here anymore. I will talk about business and developing deep relationships. My philosophy has become very simple:

> "In every situation, be thoughtful.
>
> To every living thing, be kind.
>
> You see, what matters most in life
> is not *what* we become, but *who*."

Belinda Shaw, *The Becoming of Wisdom*, p143

*If you wish to connect with Belinda, you can contact her via her email: belinda@bshawassociates.com.au*

# Just Remember Not to Give Up

James McNeil

If you had seen me just a couple of years ago, and compared that with the way I am today, you would notice a drastic difference. This is especially true if you were in my house on the night of September 10$^{th}$, 2017. I remember the date because it was that night Hurricane Irma made landfall in Florida. I was stressed, and I didn't think it was a big enough deal to warrant reaching out. Little by little, the stress crept up on me until at midnight I was sitting at my desk with a bottle of sleeping pills prescribed for me. I was debating whether or not I should take the whole bottle.

Yes, I know what that would have done to me. Oddly enough, however, that night my thoughts were not focused on dying. My thoughts were around 'going to sleep' long enough for the stress and pain to pass.

I did not take the pills.

I did finally reach out. A friend gave me the tools that night that I've been using ever since. He told me, *"Your story is not over yet."*

How did I go from there to where I am today – a confident college senior with a business and a passion for living? I need to point out before I go any further that I am by no means a professional in dealing with psychiatric issues. If you are dealing with a medical issue, please seek the help of a medical provider. I am a regular guy who was able to conquer thoughts and feelings of suicide, and this is my story of how I did it and how you can do it too.

It started with a decision. I decided to give up a few things. This runs contrary to one of the biggest lessons I remember about being successful, that we should never give up. Never give up on your dreams, your goals, and your desire to succeed. Once you give up on them, you are resigning yourself to never achieving them.

I had to take a fresh look at this concept. I believe there are some things that are worth giving up. There are things that get in the way of your journey, and these things must be given up to truly achieve the success you are seeking.

First, I had to give up self-doubt and thinking critically of myself. To explain why, I'd like to ask a question. Would you want to hang out with someone who talked about you the way you talk about yourself? Or with someone who said the things to you that you said to yourself?

In some instances, people can say yes, and to those I am thankful. I am learning day by day to be more positive to myself. I'm not saying delusional, mind you. You won't see me convincing myself that I can run a marathon. Six years in the Army took care of my knees to the point that running a marathon is out of the question, but you *will* see me rising to challenges that I had previously shied away from. One example of this is the fact that I am graduating from a prestigious university with a degree in Business Administration.

Second, I needed to give up negative thinking. While this sounds like I am repeating the first point, self-doubt is inwardly focused, while negative thinking is also outwardly focused. Self-doubt says, "I'm not able," while negative thinking tends to focus more on the situation and how the "cards are stacked against us."

Also on the "give up list" was the tendency to criticize others. Not everyone is like me. Since not everyone is like me, not everyone will do things the way I do them. Nor will they see things the way I see them. I cannot emphasize this strongly enough; there is nothing wrong with this.

It's very important to give up procrastinating as well. "I'll do it someday" needs to be replaced with "I'll do it today", or even better, "I'll do it now." Along with a fear of failure comes a fear of success. Many times, we aren't ready for success. We want to be successful, but we aren't ready for what comes with it; more responsibility among other issues for which we aren't prepared.

Finally, I needed to drop my tendency to want to make other people happy. If people are happy, we don't have as much conflict, and that sounds good. But it isn't. As Malcolm X said, "If you have no critics, you'll likely have no success." When you stand up to accomplish something, you will catch the eye of someone, and not necessarily in a good way.

If you want to be successful, giving up on your journey is not an option. There are good things to give up, however. Once you give these things up, you will find yourself much closer to the success you seek.

But that wasn't all. I had to do more than decide. To explain this, here is a riddle. Imagine one hundred frogs in a pond. Each frog is sitting on a lily pad. So, you have one hundred frogs and one hundred lily pads. Suddenly, half of the frogs decide they want to jump off their lily pad. They might want to swim, or they might even want to go for a walk. (Or would that be for a hop?) Regardless of their reason, how many are left?

You might be tempted to make this a mathematical equation and say fifty. But this is not a math problem. It isn't a math problem because none of the frogs *actually* jumped. The key is in the riddle.

"Suddenly half of the frogs *decide they want to* jump off their lily pad."

They simply decided they wanted to jump. Until they jump, their situation remains the same, and the answer to the riddle is: one hundred frogs are left.

Just like the frogs in this riddle, I had to make a decision to move forward, but it doesn't stop there. If all I did was make a decision, not much would change. My mindset might be different, but my actions remain the same. If you're 'stuck' in what you consider to be a dead-end job, deciding to look for better work does not land you a better job. Pairing that decision with action is needed.

I hit obstacles along the way, and I almost let them stop me. I had to overcome the fear of rejection. It was Sunday afternoon, and the church service had just concluded. I and several others were talking when I heard someone call out my name. I turned to see a very dear friend walking toward me. As my friend approached me, her ear-to-ear smile let me know she had good news. "James!" she exclaimed excitedly. "You won't believe this!"

"I don't know," I teased with a smile, "I might."

She rolled her eyes before continuing. "One of my instructors is looking for guest speakers!" My eyebrows went up as she continued. "Seriously! He wants to bring in guest speakers to share their experiences with his students! I know you love public speaking, so I wanted to tell you."

"Well, yes. I do have a big mouth," I responded. Ignoring her eyes rolling again, I asked for his contact information, which she gladly gave me.

The next day, I called the number. I was not prepared for the response. The person who answered was not the instructor, but his secretary. Even though it threw me off a little, I pressed forward. "Hi there. My name is James, and I am calling to ask about a program the professor is starting to bring in guest speakers—"

I was cut off. "I don't know what you're talking about." I tried to explain what I meant. It did no good. "Sir," she began derisively. "If there was a program like you're describing, I would know about it, and I don't. Have a good day," she concluded, hanging up the phone.

Somewhat awkwardly, I mumbled into the (now disconnected) phone, "Thank you for your time." To say the least, I felt defeated. You are likely nodding your head as you read this. You, too, have felt the sting of rejection. You may not have been attempting to do what I was, but the sting is the same nonetheless when you feel it.

I called a friend and mentor to ask her advice. She patiently waited while I explained what had happened, and to be honest, looking back, I can see that I was whining more than I was asking for advice. "I called to ask about a chance to speak to this professor's class, and his secretary was mean! She interrupted me and said she didn't know what I was talking about. Then she hung up on me!"

Her response cut through all of my whining and caught my attention quickly. "Will you listen to yourself?"

"What do you mean?" I moaned in response.

She went on to explain that I had let someone get to me. She asked, "Who makes the decisions on who presents in his class? Him or her?" I answered that it was most likely him, and she continued with another question. "So, she literally cannot tell you yes about speaking to his class. Correct?" I affirmed her statement, and she concluded by asking, "Why are you taking a no from someone who cannot give you a yes?"

Begrudgingly, I had to admit she had a point. I had asked someone who could not tell me yes, so the only answer she could give me was no. A little bolder now, I called back. She recognized my number in the caller ID.

"Can I help you?" her voice dripped with sarcasm.

"I'd like to speak with the professor."

"Sir, I told you before, there is no program like this."

It took a little persuading, but she did transfer my call to his phone. I was very happy to hear that he had considered implementing the program, but he had not yet told his secretary about it. I did have the opportunity to speak to his class, and it went well, but it might not have happened if I had simply taken a no. It might not have happened if I'd stopped at the first obstacle.

So, I had decided to drop the old bad habits and strike out toward a new goal. I had applied for college when I hadn't stepped foot on a campus in years. However, my journey was just getting started. It was not long before I realized there were obstacles I needed to overcome.

The first was **impostor syndrome**. I had to get out of my own head and realize that I was not an impostor for having difficulties. Nor were my struggles a **sign of weakness**. Then I had to deal with **anger** issues. I was angry with myself for not achieving the goals I believed I should have achieved by my forties. I had to get my **attitude** in order. I then had to understand the importance of **planning** for the future, and I had to realize that there was only **so much time in the day** to handle the things I wanted to do.

I had to come to grips with the fact that even though I plan, **I could still fail**, and I needed to take that chance. I also had to understand **how to bounce back** when I did fail. I needed to understand that in order to be successful, I needed to **'watch success'** in other people and learn from what they were doing right. I had to revisit what it meant to be **loyal** to friends and family who slipped up, and what loyalty I needed to expect.

I needed to (*re*) learn that **you cannot pour from an empty cup**, meaning you cannot offer more than you have to offer, and you need to pour into your own life as well. It's funny that I would tell others that lesson but not use it myself. This led to understanding what it meant to have a **'good day'** when everyone around me was grumbling into their second or third cups of coffee. Finally, I faced the tendency to worry about things **out of my control**.

This list of obstacles I faced is by no means exhaustive. You may have faced other obstacles, but each of these can be faced and overcome. Just remember not to give up.


*If you wish to connect with James, you can contact him via his email: jamesmcneil72@outlook.com*

# The One Least Likely!
Marney Perna

Suicide. A tragic set of circumstances, but it is something that only happens to other people, never to your family. Until it does!

Whammy! When it visits those near and dear to you, it causes a heart wrenching ripple of shock throughout everyone. You struggle to comprehend the news, thinking that maybe you simply misunderstood or heard it wrongly.

Most people have read stories in newspapers or via the news of families being impacted by the sudden passing of loved ones. These are more likely to be high-profile people and, although tragic and upsetting, do not totally shock or traumatise you. You are removed from the immediate and personal ripple.

Our family was touched by suicide when our beloved niece, Jo, passed by her own hand. To this day, I still see the fallout and despair that this sad event created. Personally, and professionally, what I have noticed – and one of the biggest challenges I have seen others face – is the enormous feeling of guilt and anger!

Guilt! The guilt of the living, the constant search for answers that go around and around in your head, the should haves, could haves and would haves! Should I have done something? Should I have known? Should I have seen what was going on? Could I have prevented this? Couldn't someone else see what was happening and let me know? Why couldn't they have reached out for help? Would asking how they were, have made a difference? Would being closer have helped? On and on goes the search for some form of normality and understanding.

Then there is the million-dollar question: the WHY! Why didn't I see what was going on? Why wasn't I aware? Why was this person was struggling with life? Why did she do it? Why? Why? Why?

Many years ago, when our dear niece passed by her own hand, we joined the ripple club. Some say death and grieving brings a family closer, however the opposite can happen as well. The search for answers does not always bring peace and harmony, and everyone has their own way of coping and dealing with grief and loss. A startling statement that many of us made was, "Jo was never the one that you expected would do this." She wasn't the one who you kept in your 'heart eye' as a little unsettled or unstable. Many families have members who might seem morose or subject to anxiety and depression. It would make more sense if it had been them... or would it?

To this day, I still fail to understand what was in this very competent girl's mind when she made her very final decision. The shock is still rippling through our family, and although time has passed, we still think of her and go, "Oh my God, why did you do it?" Her mum really struggled and has still not found her peace with the situation. I mean, we all struggled, but her mum has fought her demons from the get-go. It is not natural that a parent should bury their child! It was not the way things should happen! She was annihilated, gutted, and bewildered, and still cannot comprehend why she didn't realize how bad things were. She had an inkling that Jo was not feeling so well, but thought it was a case of homesickness or a situation at work.

The extra burden that was faced and further exacerbated the situation was the fact that our darling niece Jo was not living in Australia at the time; she was living overseas, and we had to repatriate her body home. What a horrible experience in an already horrible situation. This also created so many extra tasks on top of trying to deal with the grief and disbelief. Also, who was to pack up all her belongings and how are we to get everything home, and who could give us answers? We all struggled to understand. Death is so very final, and yet everyday life still goes on for others. It seems so unreal and surreal. It sucks!

Jo was a lovely person, and although searching for answers to some of life's more puzzling questions, always appeared a very stable and grounded person. She came from a very close-knit family and was close to her younger sister. She loved being the fun and loving Auntie to her many nephews and nieces. She was well educated, and was a nurse by profession. Jo lived to care for others. Having nursed for many years, she made the decision to travel to Ireland to broaden her experiences and to find more solutions to what she saw were challenges within her profession. Whilst there, she also decided that she would like to incorporate naturopathy into her toolbox of caring. We talked about it before she went overseas because I was just embarking on my kinesiology training journey. We had many things in common, including a love of reading and an interest in health and wellness and natural ways to help people cope with illness and life.

Unfortunately, what she found in her quest for answers was a form of a self-help cult. She enjoyed her nursing work and her naturopathy studies and attended many different workshops and events. At one of these events, she appeared to get herself entangled into a very cult-like environment. I am not sure if Jo or anyone knew the enormity or insidious nature of the teachings, as it was on the surface considered part of her professional development. She changed from being a happy bubbly person to an introverted and sullen person as she very quickly got swept up into this toxic cult-like environment. It was within this arena that they instilled, encouraged and brainwashed her in the belief that she was no good to herself or to her family.

Back in Australia, we were totally unaware of the turmoil and trauma that was unfolding in her life. Her friends did not know about it, her family did not know about it. But it was the catalyst for her homesickness, and made her want to come home. Somehow, this insidious, toxic cult convinced her that if she came home, she was a loser, and she would never achieve her goal of being free from her demons and negative self-beliefs. The mind can be brainwashed when fed constantly with negative thoughts, lies and untruths from others. Eventually, it starts to believe them to be truths.

The tragic circumstances are that within two weeks of booking her ticket to come home, Jo decided to take her own life. Jo faced her 'Black Night of the Soul'. She did that from a place of misguided loving care, of not wanting to be a burden to her family and not wanting to be hurtful to anyone else.

I have the firm belief that she was not in her right mind. I do not think anyone who takes their life does it from a totally sane place of mind. Ironically, it appears that they are noticeably clear about how and what they are doing and why, but it makes sense to them, not to others. It is my personal conjecture that that they become very self-orientated and self-focused. They are thinking about themselves, of how they feel and the emotions of negative self-belief, not feeling worthy of living, hopelessness and being no good or a danger to others. They appear to have lost hope, and with it their own personal values and beliefs. This is not a blame statement;

it is me trying to come to grips with why a person feels so desperate and alone that to take their life is the only option.

Unfortunately, tragically, the ones that are left behind must pick up the pieces – or try to. How do you pick up those pieces and at the same time deal with the grief of loss of your loved one? That ripple goes out and around everyone, and makes life's connection unstable and insecure. It is often said that one of the few certainties in life is death, and that is not in dispute. The dispute is in the agony of when a life is cut short so young. The 'whys' become perpetual.

There is also the ongoing anger and resentment at the 'whats' and 'whys'. Sometimes, the anger stays and becomes its own toxic burden.

There are many crossroads in our lives, and we constantly make decisions to go in a particular direction. These decisions influence our journey and that of those around us. Jo had a passion for life and of caring for others. Her legacy lives on in our sharing her name, remembering her with love, and of sharing her life stories with others. Her passing is not what defines her life. It is just a part of her story.

I often 'chat' with Jo, and I am presuming that I am not alone in that. We chat about all sorts of things, and I often find myself thinking of her when considering decisions or options. She has become one of my favourite guides within Heaven's Angels. Most people talk to those who have passed, sometimes on their significant days of celebration, other times when something reminds us of them. I encourage you to chat with your loved ones often, and share thoughts and everyday common experiences with them. Our memories are gifts from a previous time that are opened as a present for this time. Smile when something pops up and reminds you of them.

It is still sucky to not have her around, but I have found my acceptance and personal peace with myself. Am I happy about it? No, not always! The ultimate choice to live or die is not always our own decision to make, and Jo made her choice; she chose to slay her demons in a very tragic way, and one hopes she has made peace with herself. Regardless of her decision and the ongoing fallout from it, she is still our beloved niece.

Professionally, I am a natural therapist, and I specialize in kinesiology for stress management and to help clients to cope with and release trauma. Clients often come to get help with coping with a tsunami of emotions and grief from the impact of the suicide of a loved one. However, in some instances, clients are feeling so overwhelmed with life that they are personally contemplating suicide. It is also often a subject that the client has never previously shared with any else. This is never taken lightly, and they are encouraged to seek immediate medical/professional help as well. This is a massive cry for help. There is no judgement, just support, guidance and trust.

Once when chatting about the subject of suicide with my elderly mum, I was very startled to hear her mention that she, also, had once contemplated suicide. She was married and had four young children under 6. She was living in a town far away from her family connections, in a place where she did not know many people and felt very isolated and useless in life. She told me she had the tablets in her hand, and as she looked up, saw us nearby. We, her children, became her link to staying. She said she could not do it to us and threw the tablets away. She also mentioned it was something she had never spoken to anyone about, as she thought she would be judged. It was something she felt she could not share with her family or church as it was considered a taboo subject and a sinful action. There was a burden of guilt and stigma associated with the "thought of doing it", the idea that she was not strong enough or capable of caring for her family. But not being able to share her worries and concerns also impacted her physical health and wellness.

So, you really do not know what or how people are feeling. You never know who could become "the one least likely". Sometimes the happiest of people are the saddest. The saddest are sometimes the strongest.

Please let go of the anger and resentment, re-discover your joy and happiness again. Searching for answers does not get you peace – peace comes from within, and from your acceptance of the cycle of life in all its forms and time frames. Talk to your loved ones, take care, and know too that **you** are loved and blessed.


*If you wish to connect with Marney, you can contact her via her email: info@kinique.com*

# The Flood Gate

Jennifer Wojtas

After a late-night drive home from their weekly ice hockey game, my husband's best mate asked numerous times why Walter was still agitated after such gruelling sessions on the ice. Walter suddenly pulled over and said frankly, "I was abused for several years by a sick clergyman when I was 10!"

A few months later, I drove Walter to his umpteenth job interview. Amongst the deafening silence on our return home, out of the blue, Walter said, "I don't want you to be upset … but I was abused for several years at school by a bastard priest." A burdening secret he had kept buried for 15 years, from both his parents and me.

Back in the '90s, PTSD treatment was predominantly available to returned servicemen, with a plethora of resources, even dedicated mental health clinics and hospitals. I never expected the next 25 years that followed would be a blur of countless appointments made with specialists trying to find any help available for surviving victims of institutional child sex abuse.

The next wave to crash into us was an imminent need for medical intervention for Walter. Exhausted after numerous calls to medicos and navigating a fragmented mental health system, a bed became available at a clinic ironically run by a religious institution. My husband and I weren't surprised when we were told it was a dedicated PTSD ward for veterans. Though apprehensive, it was our only hope, as Walter visibly began to crumble. However, Walter felt that he could not relate to the other men (all war veterans) and didn't feel safe to disclose anything at a faith-based service.

After Walter's third admission, I got a call from his psychologist advising that Walter was being "committed" and transferred to a public medical institution, involuntarily. The doctor stated that an incident had occurred, but would not elaborate. When I arrived, a clinician told me Walter had attempted to hang himself, but as he was a well-built man he fell to the ground. Thankfully, Walter survived with only a few minor injuries, but what neither of us expected was that he'd never be allowed back at their clinic. I was confused by this, and only after pushing for a direct answer did the clinic state that Walter was classed as an insurance risk to them, so they couldn't do anything more.

Walter only stayed at the public facility for a few weeks before a magistrate concluded, from the information provided in the former clinic's reports, that Walter was mentally well enough to go home! The magistrate and the clinician may have agreed – but I knew he certainly wasn't, how could I give him the psychiatric care he desperately needed at home?

"What do we do now?" I said, both of us feeling helpless after a lot of pent-up internal frustration. I parked the car at the closest McDonald's (money was extremely tight, so no food) and we sat and cried together. We had just moved again, this time into a small unit (we would end up moving 10 times during our marriage, which did take a toll). Walter was not able to hold down any job for very long as his emotion regulation was poor which caused interpersonal issues at work. The financial and mental weight on him going forward, at times, was unbearable. This resulted in me needing to be the sole income earner from that point on.

I was so frustrated by the "system" and the injustices that I yelled at him. Walter stayed silent, and just handed me a phone number for another clinic (that a nurse at the hospital's PTSD ward had given to him before he was transferred). We called her Walter's "Angel".

The lady at the other end of the phone gave me their address details, and we couldn't believe that their service was only a few minutes away from where we were parked! When we spoke to admissions (Angel #2), they asked us to drive straight there; a private clinic that could intake a small number of public patients. We went straight there, and a nurse gently took Walter to the wing that he would later end up calling "home".

This "home" saw Walter admitted almost three times a year during the following 10-year period. Our children and I celebrated many birthdays, Christmases and special events at the clinic as his visitors. During these stays, my husband agreed that electroconvulsive therapy (ECT) treatments were a safer and more hopeful option for treatment of his PTSD. Regrettably, after countless sessions, his memory was never the same, and his PTSD remained, if not worsened.

Our family home was too foreign for Walter now. He had become institutionalised, in a sense, so whenever he came home to us (from being in a controlled hospital environment) he would relapse and go back to the clinic shortly after. Triggers surrounded Walter daily from all types of media, especially during the royal commission into child abuse, so each day at home on his own was a challenge. That RC was a true blessing for victim survivors, but it was a huge shame that the flow-on effect was that survivors could not fully escape their enduring trauma from flashbacks and triggers, some lifelong. I tried to help Walter manage these triggers by reading the synopses on movies, newspapers, mags, books and DVDs beforehand. My radar was always on, and I tried everything I could to manage his environment for as long as I could.

On one occasion, one of our teenagers arrived home before I did and had to kick in the bedroom door to get to him (too graphic to describe) and suffered a panic attack, not able to dial 000. Luckily, I arrived just after garaging the car, and called the ambulance, but moreover, I was devastated for what my child had witnessed firsthand.

On another occasion, Walter had overdosed just before we were due to arrive home from work, and again – just in time – the same teen and I walked in to find him struggling to breathe, and we were able to ring an ambulance. We made excuses to the neighbours that Walter had heart issues to stop our nosey neighbours from knowing what was really happening.

3-4 months later, he made his 3rd attempt at home with another medication overdose – I had gone to bed early that night. Thankfully, my intuition suddenly woke me up. I walked through the unit to find Walter slumped at the dining table. I franticly called an ambulance, who took us to the closest public hospital, and Walter was placed in an induced coma to keep him alive.

The following fortnight was horrific, with daily visits to ICU with the girls. Soul-shattering helplessness blanketed me until I went into autopilot, barely speaking to the girls as I was merely coping and not actually functioning or looking after myself. I couldn't fix anything, everything was out of my control, and I had no idea if Walter would make it. Miraculously, Walter survived (I was convinced he had nine lives) but from that point on, we had no idea what would come next after being so close to losing him again.

The torment of wanting to be home with him to save him from himself mixed with the immense financial pressure to keep working so the bills could be paid. Unfortunately, in mid-2014, I experienced an injury at work which resulted in undergoing many surgeries over the next few years. I accepted a redundancy from work during this time, which helped us make the decision to pack up everything and move. With the kids in Sydney, we decided on a few hours north to be debt-free and experience a somewhat calmer life. A new beginning for us, and hopes of some peace, surrounded by nature.

Within 12 months we managed to move, and just as we moved in, my only sibling passed away from brain cancer. A few months later, I needed to look after my own health; my physical pain was taking a toll, and I needed to put myself first — something that I'd not been able to do for decades. More surgery was performed back in Sydney. I was lucky to be supported by my eldest daughter during this time away from Walter. She was marvellous in spreading her time out travelling up to visit her father to check in on him, as by then he had advanced Parkinson's and was completely housebound. Our other daughter was holidaying overseas in the US at the time, so we were all in different locations. In hindsight, this seemed like a perfect storm for Walter.

On the Friday before Father's Day 2017, all my medical reports seemed positive, and I'd spoken with the kids and Walter each day whilst recovering in Sydney. My eldest daughter had taken one of her children to surprise Walter, unannounced, and she described his demeanour as unusually calm and happy to see them.

The next two days was radio silence from Walter. We always knew that if he were angry about something, he would ignore us for a few days, but would always be over it by the 3rd day. It was a definite pattern with him over the years. Walter would even light-heartedly joke about it with our eldest daughter, saying, "I know if you don't hear from me, you'll make a fuss and call Police to check on me."

I was still in hospital on total bed rest and had no vehicle to drive myself home if needed. Our daughter sent a message to Walter to say if he didn't reply, she would be calling an ambulance immediately (this would be a sure-fire way to get him to respond). With still no reply, she contacted the ambulance to do an urgent welfare check at the house. A paramedic called her back to say they are en route and will ring her with an update ASAP.

After two gruelling hours, she did receive that call … but from a Senior Constable from the police that attended, to say he was inside the property, but deceased. My eldest daughter had the dreadful task of calling me at the hospital to let me know that her father, my husband of 40 years, was indeed at our new home, but he wouldn't be there when I got back. The only comfort was that the officer described him looking "peaceful" in his favourite armchair, in front of the lounge room TV, where he liked to be.

The next morning my daughter met me at the hospital where I discharged myself so that we could identify Walter at forensics together. The task of calling my other daughter in the US in the car, a phone call no-one ever wants to or even knows how to make, fell to me. We made our way to the Newcastle Hospital coroner's office to have our interviews and to say our very last goodbyes. Both of us still couldn't believe it was him in that room. It couldn't be, surely he had another life left...

With the support of my girls and extended family and friends, I'm a little bit closer to achieving Walter's wishes of living my life without the constant worry. It's bittersweet when things feel calmer, and I'm learning to give myself permission to look forward to some things again and enjoy time with our grandkids, even knowing that he isn't physically with us to do the same. The waves of grief that only a few short years ago would knock me off my feet every day have decreased over time. Presently, it's equally beautiful and painful to appreciate how words, sounds, smells, food, songs, places, photos and memories can open the flood gates again, and the tears of my undying love for him surely follow.

RIP WRW – 3/9/17

Now forever at Peace.

# Forever In My Heart

Marthie Talu

My journey began in late November 2008, when I received a phone call from my mother telling me that my brother Tinus has committed suicide. It was instant shock and disbelief; my mind could not understand what I was being told.

It was a day just like any other – only thing is Tinus did not show up at work as usual, and nobody could get a hold of him. My younger brother Marius went to have a look for him, and he was the one who found him. On the edge of the beach, people had already started to gather around. Marius took him in his arms, trying to shield him from all the onlookers.

We lost a lot that day, everyone did. Tinus had his own second-hand motor dealership and employed a couple of people, including my brother Marius. He also provided a place to stay for my mother and brother. He had taken Marius under his wing and tried to teach him the business.

We were a close-knit family; we did not have much, but we had a roof over our heads, and my parents made sure there was always food on the table. The situation prompted my brothers to get jobs at around the age of 16. There was not money to go and study, and each one had to work to be able to study further. Kobus, the eldest, fixed cars; Fanus studied electronics at the local TAFE; Tinus went on to university and studied accounting; Marius had dyslexia, so he went straight to work; and I studied communication. My father worked as a distribution manager Monday to Friday, and my mother worked as the fruit and vegetable manager at the local supermarket Monday to Saturday.

Religion played a big part in our upbringing. As kids, we all had to go to church on Sundays and then stayed further for bible studies. We were all baptised and had to take communion, and were presented to the church at age 16.

Fanus and Tinus had to go to military training, as it was a requirement of the government of the time. They had to do two years and spend some time on the border wars. Later in life, my mother told me that Tinus was struggling with some of the experiences he had to endure. He was bullied by a higher ranked official and ended up in the infirmary with exhaustion and heat stroke. On another occasion, they had to drive over bodies with an armoured vehicle. That stayed with him all his life.

I grew up the youngest of 5 kids, and my mother made sure we were all up to date with what was happening with each of us. We lost my dad in 2004 due to a heart attack. I got married and moved away with my husband. My youngest brother Marius took care of my mother and started working for Tinus. The others had their own lives and children to look after, but we all kept in touch.

Tinus always liked the finer things in life. He loved to socialise and be a valued member of the community. Once I broke one of his wine glasses, and I had to replace it with 6 of the same. He was always there for the family, a great problem solver, and probably the only person who got the tax commissioner to personally present him with a cheque for the money they owed him.

Tinus always had a bad temper; even as a baby he would argue with anyone, and we accepted him like that. He hated the fact that there was never enough money, and was motivated to make something of himself. He did not finish his degree, but started working as an accountant in a local company that manufactured heavy machinery for the mining industry. He worked hard and moved up in the company. After a couple of years, he decided to quit and start his own HR business.

Over time he had a couple more businesses that each time ended in failure, causing him to start from nothing again. In his last business he had a second-hand motor dealership that was situated near the coast. He had plenty of deals going, and was waiting for one to go through. He must have panicked, thinking he would lose everything again.

Things like suicide don't just happen, and when you think back on everything, you realise that there were signs that they were planning this for some time. In Tinus's case, he kept a reasonable amount of cash at home and invested in insurance policies to take care of his wife and my mother. He left a detailed will, making his wife and my mother beneficiaries. I remember once when he organised for Marius and my mother to video chat me in Australia for more than two hours. At that time, phoning overseas was still expensive. Then there was the time he spent with Marius to teach him the business. We did not think anything of it at the time, but as they say, hindsight is always 2020.

What hit me the hardest was the fact that I could not attend the funeral; we were living 10,000 kilometres away. I could not be there for my mother and my family, and had to grieve all by myself. I had to rely on my mother and brothers to tell me what happened.

This was not the only loss I had to deal with all by myself; we lost Fanus in 2014, Kobus in 2015, and finally my mother in November of 2015. This left only Marius and me.

One of greatest lessons I think I learnt during this time is that life goes on, and it's important to celebrate those you have with you and those who have passed. They are not gone; they just live on in a different reality, and do come and visit sometime. They will always look after you without you realising it. Celebrate them, do the things that they love to do. Cook a meal that they love, visit their favourite places.

I got through this and all the other losses I experienced by focusing on what is important in that instant. I had plenty of distraction, with a young son to look after, and later, a daughter. Live each day as best you can. I also tried to understand all the facts surrounding his death. Speaking to relatives and getting their take on his death helped me come to terms with it.

After all this, I think the one thing I have not been taught by my parents is how to live without them. Grief is a process; allow yourself to go through all seven stages. Talk to people on how you feel. Nothing brings a family together more than death; it shows you what is really important in life.

It does get better with time, but like with me after the loss of Tinus, I got sent a photograph of him a couple of months later and I just burst out in tears. Maybe I needed that to let go of all the pent-up emotion.

Each of us copes differently with death, and when it happens in such a horrific way, we need to process the information. Take your time, it not a race. It might not make sense at the time, but later you will realise why it happened and that you could not have stopped it no matter what you did.

Tinus was only 45 when he died, and I can't help but wonder what his future would have been like. Maybe he would have immigrated, like me. His death left a hole in my heart and a void in our whole family. My kids grew up never knowing him, and I think they would have benefited greatly by having him as part of their lives.

All I know is that I still love him as my brother, and I am grateful for the time I got to spend with him. He will be forever in my heart.

# The Dragonfly

Once, in a little pond, in the muddy water under the lily pads, there lived a little water beetle in a community of water beetles. They lived a simple and comfortable life in the pond with few disturbances and interruptions.

Once in a while, sadness would come to the community when one of their fellow beetles would climb the stem of a lily pad and would never be seen again. They knew when this happened; their friend was dead, gone forever.

Then, one day, one little water beetle felt an irresistible urge to climb up that stem. However, he was determined that he would not leave forever. He would come back and tell his friends what he had found at the top.

When he reached the top and climbed out of the water onto the surface of the lily pad, he was so tired, and the sun felt so warm, that he decided he must take a nap. As he slept, his body changed and when he woke up, he had turned into a beautiful blue-tailed dragonfly with broad wings and a slender body designed for flying.

So, fly he did! And, as he soared he saw the beauty of a whole new world and a far superior way of life to what he had never known existed.

Then he remembered his beetle friends and how they were thinking by now he was dead. He wanted to go back to tell them, and explain to them that he was now more alive than he had ever been before. His life had been fulfilled rather than ended.

But, his new body would not go down into the water. He could not get back to tell his friends the good news. Then he understood that their time would come, when they, too, would know what he now knew. So, he raised his wings and flew off into his joyous new life!

~Author Unknown~

With Compliments,

www.kinique.com

'Uniquely for you' change your life today!

# My Date with Suicide
## Stella Rae

The day started with me getting ready for work. I showered, put my face on and got dressed. I gave my dog some water and went to work. My workday went as usual. Drove to my clients' homes, assisted my clients with hygiene, palliative care, social support. And then I came home. But coming home was not like any other day I had experienced, as after work I had to visit the police station. On Australia Day 2020, I met my threshold; I just didn't know it until it happened.

The IT happening... well, it was a compilation of events that led up to this moment in time, so I will give you a brief rundown.

In July 2018, the love of my life came home and said he "can't live with me any longer". I looked at him, trying to hold myself together but shattering into a million pieces on the inside.

A couple of days, later I was terminated from my job for "abusing" a resident. On this same day, I had spent the afternoon in a photoshoot for a belated Mother's Day present with my daughter. Oh, she is so beautiful.

I had this gorgeous friend who came up to visit me to pull me out of my dark space, as I felt like the world had just been ripped out beneath me. She told me that I needed to stand up and be the fighter she knew I was.

So, in the last few months of 2018, I fought for my life. I was told by Centrelink to go to unfair dismissal, and I won. It took about 2 months of gathering information to figure out that these 3 women had indeed committed fraud and falsified documents of complaint(s). They were accusing me of doing things outside of my scope, or being with clients that I never looked after; apparently, I was getting in trouble for things that happened on days when I didn't even work. They planned it, as I had witnessed a cover-up of a death of an elderly resident and they knew it. After I won and got paid out and had my termination reversed and turned into a resignation, I found out that they all "resigned". Not! The company knew they had done the wrong thing, and they were damn lucky I had been too shattered on a personal level to take it to court.

During this process, I chose to live with the man who shattered my heart, and seek counselling. And my grief came up fiercely; there was no escaping this, for at this time in my life, I had nothing to do but grieve. I asked the father of my kids to look after our children, as I was becoming aware that this person whom I loved was not who I thought he was. I had no job. So, when he went to work, my grief switched on like clockwork. I would force myself to eat, I would watch YouTube videos – mainly "The Greatest Showman" rehearsals and the Galen Hooks choreography "River" and sometimes I'd dance to it in my underwear and high heels whilst no one was watching. But as I did this, my soul crumbled. I would fall to my knees and cry for what felt like an eternity, and would try and cook food and fall on the tiles and sob for hours. I would feel my legs give way in the shower, and would grab onto the shower walls for dear life as this river poured out of me.

I got to a point at close to 3 months of this daily occurrence where I realised that I was no longer grieving for this man – I was grieving for everything I had not given myself permission to grieve for. The abuse I suffered as child, being sexually abused by an uncle, being raped at

15, and being drugged and gang raped by a couple, resulting in a miscarriage. I lost a baby. I was grieving for the loss of my marriage. Grieving for the loss of my many jobs because I made a stand for what's right, for justice for my clients, and for myself. Grieving for not being able to be the mother to my children that they needed, desired, as I seemed to always be in conflict. God damn, I have tried to just be the best person I could. Stand up for those with no voice; stand up for those that struggled to do this on their own; just stand up for what's damn right.

So, whilst I grieved and went through this unfair dismissal process, I sought some professional assistance – a naturopath and some energy work. This was to assist with the deep emotional heartbreak I was feeling, and as I poured my heart out to these women, I was smashed in the face with the words "Domestic Violence". These words stung my ears like nothing I had heard before. I wasn't having a bar of it. A huge part of me went into denial, even though this other little part *knew* this shit was going down. This little part helped me through these months of denial and grief and fighting an unfair dismissal, and my eyes were opening up to this man that I thought I knew.

Although our relationship had ended, I quickly figured out that I was stuck in this position in my life – no job, no money – so that I could see who this man truly was. During these months, god, the shit that I accomplished; writing it all down here right now, I'm like, I did *what* now?

I had gone to see a lawyer about a property settlement, as this man had told me about all of his savings and how he and his dad had $100k together, and I looked at my financial status and I was way over my head in debt. Knocked back. This came out in my counselling sessions, and it was yet another slap in the face; you have been

Forever Changed by Suicide

financially abused. Noooo! Oh god! I remember just sinking in my chair and getting hit with this domestic violence stuff over and over again. Gaslighting, emotional abuse, psychological abuse, and even sexual abuse.

I remember looking at him and, at some stage, wondering who the fuck he was! Did I have a blindfold on? For a whole 10 years? Then it became clear – he had me right at the beginning, where he made sure I knew that he could "kill with his bare hands and not leave a mark". The rest was easy. He said jump, I jumped. He said he had no money, I paid. He shifted my stuff round the house, and then would tell me that I should put it in the same place and I wouldn't forget. I would have to text him when I finished work, tell him wherever I was, and for how long.

Then in November, a week before I was secretly planning to leave the house, he pushed me. He actually laid his hands on me, and pushed me out of the way. I could see he was coming undone as I had caught on to his game. I packed up and made my escape. I thought I had the best plan; I was sure he had no clue. I got my boxes and my clothes, a man and his van, my mechanic, and my daughter's boyfriend at the time. We did it. I cleaned the house and took photos, as my name was on the lease and I was still liable.

Little did I know how evil this man was. He broke into my new house and swapped a remote over. He stalked me on dating sites, and just happened to drive round the corner as I sat down with a guy, and then actually cat fished me into meeting someone that wasn't there whilst he was across the street, watching. I was also meeting up with him, as for some strange reason it gave me a sense of safety if I knew where he was. I was definitely safer. This came to a crashing halt when I caught wind of him playing me. Like, I'd already had my suspicions, but this concreted it. He was coercing his co-worker, and sleeping with me.

I filed a protection order against him the next year. He stalked me, hacked my accounts – anything on our property settlement with a DV lawyer, he hacked. The more I followed instruction by Centrelink and financial counsellors, the more deceit I uncovered about him. He'd had access to my Facebook Messenger for eighteen months. He had hour long phone calls with our female neighbour almost daily. He was sending nasty messages about me to his sister, and she talked about me like I was a bludging no-hoper. He set up a secret email, and inside of it, to my disgust, was a Switzerland porn dating site with his disgusting fetishes and a picture of my vagina.

Hypervigilance had set in good and proper and I found myself breaking down in my car, realising I hadn't told him of my whereabouts, only to realise I wasn't with him any longer. I couldn't shop, as I was waiting for him to tell me what to buy; I couldn't cook, as I heard him critique me every time I picked up the knife.

Before all this, things had settled down from about April through to September; a massive thank-you to my daughter, her boyfriend, and a friend at the time (although I felt like I lived in a frat house with three grown teenagers). They saved me with their support, love and care.

Then I met this guy. And I *so* did not want a relationship, and I told him of this, but he wasn't having a bar of it. He wanted me. The night after we first kissed, and I dropped him to his bike, we had messaged each other "goodnight" only for me to be woken by his call at midnight saying he was in my street, waking my neighbours and trying to find me. It was the middle of the fucking night. I was like, "Well, don't think you're getting a booty call, I have work." He said he "just wanted to hold me". I was like, "Whatever." That day I had a split shift, but he wanted to take me for a ride on his bike. I said I would let him know when I was home. He replied, "All good, your flatmate let me in." I'm shaking my head going, "What the...?" He wanted me to agree to tell him if I kiss anyone else. I'm like, "We kissed last night, dude, and you want a signed contract from me?" We went for a short ride, and then I had to go back to work; he said that when I finished work, he needed to talk to me. He came over and told me he was going to try one last stint with his wife, take some ICE and get the truth from her. I told him to go for it. I didn't have a single bit of attachment for him at this stage.

This was short-lived; I had a message four days later, and within two weeks of texting I caved and met him at his house and met his daughters. Then my world changed forever. I had three weeks of bliss. This man swept me off my feet, and I was trying to hold back as I didn't want to rush ... and then it was all over. He ended it three weeks later because I had not replied to his texts in a timely manner – twenty minutes.

We texted for a couple of days after that, and I went to his house. He got really angry with me, and I tried to leave but he wouldn't let me. I tried for hours and finally got away, while but driving I was petrified that he was following me, and got my daughter's best friend to lock up the house.

Yes, I went back. Oh, the hindsight. The next few months played out in a series of drinking together, him accusing me of sleeping with the seventeen-year-old in my house and sleeping around, him cussing at me, saying, "You slut", "Paedophile", "Piece of trash", "Whore". Shaming me publicly on Facebook, humiliating me to his family, children and friends, and then making public scenes whilst out where I was escorted by security to safety whilst he puffed up and shamed me to whoever would listen. I even had to be rescued by my children after I was drugged at his house.

So, in mid-January this came to a screaming halt and it ended as I decided to spend the day with a friend, and I woke up to him showing me pictures of his online dating efforts. This hurt like a knife through my heart.

This is when I applied for a protection order against him following all the public scenes, the threats to the seventeen-year-old; the list goes on. Unfortunately for me, a few days after, I called him after a night out with my friends and unbeknownst to me he recorded twenty minutes from a thirty-minute phone call where he was asking me to come over. He set me up. I had a video on me the minute I got to his house, which resulted in me being taken home in a police car and him using this video to manipulate, intimidate and harass me during the court proceedings.

Then I went to get smokes one night, and lo and behold, the *other* ex was outside my house. Parked. I froze in fear. I called the police and reported it. We had our arbitration the next day.

A week and half later, it was Australia Day, and I was enjoying the day and having drinks. By late in the evening, I was asked to leave a premise due to being drunk. No worries, I went and sat on the wall outside. But police got called to another matter nearby; it clearly had been a rough day for them, and they decided to extradite some rules and I was their prey. They asked me to leave as it was a licensed premise. I said no, as I had a friend inside and was waiting for them so that they didn't go home alone. This situation went from bad to worse, as they then said, "If you don't leave, I will have to force you." In that moment I knew I was in trouble, and so were they. I begged them not to touch me, as I knew that I couldn't handle a man touching me. Next thing I knew I was thrashing for my life, thrown to the ground, handcuffed and taken to the watch house. Again, another trip home in the police van. But when I got home, I was angry, and I just lost my shit, grabbing anything I could grab and throwing it around the house. I grabbed the car keys and attempted to drive to shops for smokes, but was stopped by the kids. They left in the car and I slept off the anger and drunkenness, and I woke the next day trying to recall why everything went so bad.

This led me to my date with suicide. I went to the police station and the impact of what had gone on hit me. I had been arrested. I had my fingerprints recorded, my photos taken. I apologised to the officer for what had happened to the officers on duty that night. I got home, and the teenagers had taken their furniture. Everything was gone.

I fell into a heap on the tiled floor and cried and cried. My dog Freya tried to comfort me, and then a strange calmness came over me and I knew what to do. I got up, checked the cupboards for pills. None. Ok, I will go to the shop. My daughter came for a chat and wanted to join me, but I sent her away. I drove to the shop and I bought the strongest over-the-counter painkiller in the chemist, and then about 4 packets of Panadol and Nurofen from the supermarket – I went through self-serve to avoid raising suspicion. I came home, popped all the pills into a bowl, and sat down outside with a pen and paper, gin & coke and the tablets. I pushed two tablets and tried to chase them. My body repelled them, and I gagged. So, I did one by one for hours with the gin & coke, and wrote my goodbye letters. I could feel my body slowing down, so I finished up writing and took my bowl of tablets and chaser drink to bed and continued there until I fell asleep.

Four hours or so later, I woke up. Well, I was fuming. I was so god damn angry that I woke up; it was like 2:30am and I needed to vent. I called a couple of the lifeline numbers, only to be put through the "press this button" process, which just made me angrier. Then I got through on a line. Poor girl... I gave it to her, and sobbed and cried, and was petrified of how I would tell my work. The shame had wrapped me up like a cocoon. And then there was a knock at the door. The police, doing a welfare check. I just finished saying everything on the phone, then I had to repeat myself to the police, and I was so exhausted. Then another knock, the ambulance. And luckily, the police briefed them for me, and they asked what and where the tablets were and then walked me to the ambulance. I was admitted to the emergency ward where they checked my bloods. I had indeed taken too many, and was now under their mandatory care for 36 hours and had to have my attempt reversed.

I told barely anyone until 9 months later. And here I am, sharing this in a book.

# The Sins of the Fathers
Mary Wong

Have you ever wondered why? Searched for answers about what makes people treat a child a certain way... or even what made you respond the way you did?

I did.

From the moment I started school, I couldn't work out why some of the teachers were so mean — most of them, actually. The only one that wasn't mean was the young one, newly qualified. The others were around my mother's age, and seemed to have just decided I was scum. They took every opportunity to ridicule me, to insinuate I was somehow unworthy, their behaviour enabling my fellow students to treat me similarly.

It formed a pattern of behaviour that shaped me throughout my first 40+ years. Then, damaged by the trauma of the bullying and a long series of subsequent events, and coupled with post-natal depression, I figured the only way out was *out*.

In a moment of clarity, an awful realisation struck. I was not only considering taking myself out, but also taking my children.

That moment saved my life.

That moment was the one when I reached out and started my journey to recovery, and the journey of campaigning for others to reach out for support through conversation. The journey was long and convoluted — it involved a lot of therapy followed by a lot of study and many years of reflection, meditation, and self-work. I needed to understand the *why* of human behaviour. It involved learning to be brave, to embrace vulnerability, and to speak publicly about my journey as part of reaching others with a message of hope.

As part of my recovery, I attended a kinesiologist who identified an issue with rejection that arose around two years of age. As the youngest of six children, born over eight years, I assumed it would have been around the time I started getting into everyone else's things and becoming annoying to them, so it made sense to me.

As my recovery progressed, I felt compelled to help others who were struggling emotionally and studied counselling. As part of that study, I was required to ask questions about my family history.

What I learnt stunned me.

"Since you are asking, there's something I have to tell you – something that has to be shared. I don't want to take it to the grave with me," Mum said.

Intrigued, I leaned in to listen. Was I about to learn the big family secret she had alluded to many years prior?

"What is it?"

"I need to tell you about Pop and what happened to him."

My mum had a tough childhood. When she was just 6, her father died of a heart attack in his thirties, a legacy of the bends from his work as a bridge footings diver as a younger man. It was just prior to 1940, and no social assistance was available. The second oldest of five children, mum and her 8-year-old sister were responsible for caring for the younger ones while their mother went out to clean houses so they could afford to eat. The baby was just 2.

Less than two years later, the baby died of tetanus. The grief-stricken family continued, through the Second World War, a widow and her four remaining children barely scraping together enough to get by. My mother finished school in her early teens and was sent to work to supplement the family income as in-home help for a disabled woman.

After the war finished, things started to pick up for the family. Mum's paternal uncle returned from the war and, as was often the custom back then, took on the care of his late brother's family, marrying mum's mother. Out of respect for their late father, the family called him "Pop", a name that stayed with him for the rest of his years.

Mum describes him as a good man – a hard worker – quirky, but very caring. He was a bootmaker by trade and would craft sturdy leather boots on his lasts and machines under the house. He didn't go out much, but when he did, he always carried a rope and a knife in his pocket. Nobody knew why, or what they were for. He had come back from the war, suffering from what was called "shell-shock". We now call it PTSD. The culture back then was to sweep problems under the rug – don't talk about it, and it won't exist.

So, nobody addressed their concerns.

And one day, after the children had married and were no longer in need of him to raise them, he took himself away from the family home to a public park and used the rope to end his life. The youngest in my family, I was about two at the time. My older siblings remember him as a kind and loving man. They were not made aware of what happened to him, only that he was gone.

After mum told me what happened, she was quiet, lost in her reflections. I was too in-the-moment to make the connection between this tragic event and my own life journey. It was only later – some months later in fact – that it hit me. The rejection I felt as a two-year-old was due to the grief the others were feeling. It wasn't about me at all! For years I had blamed myself for my behaviour, accepting that I was a pest and annoying to be around.

The rejection I had experienced was the thing that made me try desperately to get attention as a young child. It was the thing that made me a precocious, loud child when I started school. The loudness was the thing that made the teacher name-call me "Miss Know-it-all" when I answered questions she had asked, desperate to impress. And it was the catalyst for all the events that followed, eventuating in a combination of post-natal depression and PTSD from a childhood bullying incident involving guns. It was the catalyst for me almost ending my own life.

The biblical metaphor was my living experience – the sins of the father playing out upon his family – the very family he had loved and nurtured; the ones he would never wish to hurt. That's the thing about suicide – the thing I often find myself explaining to others. When one is in the position of considering suicide, it's usually not with the intent to hurt others. More often than not, the suicidal person truly believes the world would be better off without them.

The way your thoughts work when you are in that space is not rational – it seems so clear at the time, but the thinking behind the decisions made is badly flawed.

Pop's decision to suicide in a public park would have been in consideration for his family – to protect them from finding him in the family home and needing to deal with the outcome. And yet, it was the very thing that created a stigma for the family – the stigma of mental health issues is still alive and well today, but only a fraction of what it was back then.

The teachers who judged and treated us cruelly in our childhood knew what had happened. The whole family was judged on Pop's actions. As a very empathic child, I felt that judgement very strongly wherever I went but had no idea what it was about. The sense that there was something "wrong" about our family followed us everywhere. If Pop had been in a place where he was able to think rationally, if he had been given the support he needed, he would never have done something that affected his family so badly.

I have spoken of my darkness, and I speak only of myself. I know I am not the only member of my family who has struggled with this demon, but that is their story to tell – their personal journey of recovery and I will not speak of it for them.

What I *will* speak of is how we as a family could have helped each other, if only we had known how.

What we needed to do was to talk about it; develop an understanding of our grief, our shock, our loss; to have a realisation of how important it is to be kind to ourselves; to live in an environment of acceptance. In doing that, we would have been able to support each other, to bond more deeply in our grief, to become stronger, more resilient.

But we were silent.

So silent, that a whole family's lack of awareness created a situation where members of that family have come close to repeating the tragedy.

To this day, I thank God for my moment of clarity.

As a method of self-preservation, I had learned to stay silent, to not speak out about my issues.

That was the very thing that nearly killed me.

I sought help only when in that moment I realised I was thinking of hurting someone other than myself.

Without that realisation, I would have stayed silent.

The silence around suicide stems from the stigma of mental illness. The judgement by society, and the self-judgement that comes with this struggle, are key causative components of the silence. Family members of those who have suicided are statistically at a higher risk of themselves suiciding – it is a devastating, vicious cycle.

The cycle must be broken.

And it can be – through open and honest conversation.

The issue is, while conversation is a natural part of life, we often have no understanding of how to approach the difficult subjects. In my counselling and Conversational Intelligence® coaching, I often meet with people who walk on eggshells around someone they love, never addressing key issues, because they are scared it will all go horribly wrong if they do.

It's destructive behaviour, and it continues the cycle of devastation.

The exciting part is that these skills can be learned – we have the perfect opportunity to break the cycle.

In my work, I mentor and teach people the skills to create a safe and supportive environment, where the conversations of support are enabled; where supporters know how to ask the right questions so that people are empowered to reach out; and where those same supporters know how to assist those who need help to find the kind of support that is right for them.

Reaching out for help is often seen as an admission of weakness – but in fact it is a move of great strength and courage.

Fearlessness is not only the ability to boldly step into the light.

True fearlessness requires you to embrace both light and dark; to be prepared to also step into the dark, allowing yourself to take the step without knowing the outcome – to be in a space of absolute vulnerability. It takes courage to do that, and when we encourage people to safely go into that space, we support them to unlock the cell of pain in which they are imprisoned.

Our leaders need to know and understand what is needed. Our teachers, our managers, our influencers all need to learn the skills and to create a world where we stop judging ourselves and others for shortcomings, and in doing so, lead all humans along a road to safety.

Every human is flawed in some way or another, and it is in that flawed design that we are absolutely perfect.

There is no need for judgement, and every reason for acceptance.

Conversations in a space of acceptance, non-judgement and support will break the cycle.

It's time to talk.


*If you wish to connect with Mary, you can contact her via her email:*
*mary@optimalcoaching.com.au*

# Touched by Suicide

Rita-Marie Lenton

Suicide has personally touched me twice in my lifetime.

To understand how, I would have to go back to when I was a young girl.

My second cousin, Teddy, was a very big part of my growing up from a really young age. His mother, my great Aunt Alice, had a hand in raising me when I was around one year old.

I remember when we moved back home to live at my great grandmother's house. My cousin Margaret (from a different aunt) and Teddy used to come and take me to the movies.

I knew Teddy was a horseman and rode in rodeos all over the countryside. His father was a drover, and they were often on the road. So, Uncle Pat, Teddy and his brothers came in and out of our family's life over the years.

Aunty Alice died when I was about six. I still remember the visits to the hospital and sitting on her bed and chatting to her.

Skip forward a few more years and I am now nine years old. I can remember the adults of the household speaking in hushed tones and us children being sent outside to play. We were not allowed to go back inside the house until we were called. So, here we were, my older brother and our two younger sisters and me, all outside playing in the dirt. All the time wondering what the hell was going on.

All of a sudden, my brother jumped up and said stay here; next minute, I could see him standing on the forty-four-gallon drum that we had near one of our windows. He jumped on the drum, and as the window was open, he could hear what the adults were talking about.

He was there for a little while, then came back to where my sisters and I were playing. He had tears running down his face, and he said that Teddy was dead. I looked at him with disbelief, and felt myself leave my own body. I was stunned. What did he mean, Teddy was dead? He can't be!

Not long after that, we were allowed back inside. My mother was crying, her friends were trying to console her and, as children, we didn't quite understand. Then, my stepfather explained that Ted had shot himself. Still, my young mind wasn't registering what the hell was going on. As usual, it fell to me to make sure my younger sisters were fed and put to bed.

The funeral was held about two weeks later. All the adults went, and of course, we stayed home; kids didn't go to funerals in those days. I know my mother held on to a lot of anger regarding the death and wanted to blame others for what had happened.

It wasn't until four years later, around thirteen years old, that I learnt from my Uncle Patty what really happened. I don't believe I was meant to know; he was drunk, and I was trying to put him to bed for mum when he started talking. He seemed to be pleading with his son, saying over and over, "Put the gun down, boy, put the gun down." When I asked my mum what he meant, she told me that my Uncle Patty was facing Ted, pleading with him to put the gun down, when Ted put the gun into his mouth and pulled the trigger.

Having lost one of my best friends in a car accident when I was seven, and of course my Aunty Alice and my great grandmother, I knew all about death from a young age, and I understood that our loved ones were not here anymore. I never really understood, though, someone taking their own life.

Fast forward to the year 1992. Our phone was ringing – it was three in the morning, and you have to know that something is not quite right. My husband had jumped out of bed – something that was unusual for him – he felt he had to be the one to get the phone. As I came out of the bedroom, I could see him rocking and crying and saying, "No! No! No!"

I tried to take the phone from him; he resisted at first, but then he let me have the phone. It was his mother, telling us that his brother had taken his and his children's lives in Western Australia. I will not go into details as they were horrific; I was stunned and upset, but I realised that I had bigger problems to deal with. I had a husband who had gone into complete shock – he couldn't move from where he was sitting. It took a while, but I got him to the lounge chair, where he stayed for the next twenty-four hours. Once the sun rose, I rang his work to let them know that he wouldn't be in as his brother had passed away. Robin, his friend and colleague, rang him, and David told him what had happened as Robin had met Dave's brother the week before, when he had come to visit us.

I heard David say, "No! I don't want to see anyone!" as he hung up. It would have been about two hours later that Robin was at our door saying to me, "I don't care what he said. I'm here."

I was so grateful, as it gave me time to breathe. Robin walked through the door and sat on the lounge with Dave and just held him without saying a word. Robin stayed with Dave for the rest of the day and night.

The day after we heard the news, we received the letter that had been posted to us; Dave's brother had written three letters. One to his mate, one to his mother, and one to us.

In the letter to us, he thanked us for having him in our home the week before, then he went on to offer apologies to me for doing this around the time of my birthday. We had received the letter on my birthday.

As we read the letter, it started to explain a few of small little quirks about Dave's brother we noticed but didn't put much thought into at the time (oh, hindsight is a bloody wonderful thing). He explained that, because of his personal situation, he had made up his mind to come and say goodbye, and there could be no turning back. He had reached his point of no return in a marriage breakup.

I don't, for one minute, condone what happened, and I am still having trouble trying to understand. As we had just bought our new home, we didn't have the money to go over to WA to any funeral, not that he got one – his wife wouldn't do it, and I cannot blame her.

Moving on into my now chosen career as a funeral director, having had these experiences in my personal life has really given me a greater understanding of families and what they are going through when someone takes their own life.

I can never answer why this happens. From both of my experiences, I have just learned that the person is in a very dark place, at a point of no return. With my cousin, his father standing in front of him and trying to get the gun off him didn't stop the end result. This is the guilt my uncle lived with for the rest of his days. His nightmares were a testimony to this.

With my brother-in-law, my husband begged him to stay in Queensland and not go back to WA. The guilt both my husband and I felt took us a long time to get over, as we saw the signs but were so wrapped up in ourselves that we didn't realise what they meant. At the end of the day, we could not have stopped what had happened. It was something that was out of our control. The only thing that kept me sane during those months was saying the Lord's Prayer, and the line from the Bible when Jesus was on the cross: "Father, forgive them, for they know not what they do."

*If you wish to connect with Rita-Marie, you can contact her via her email: ritamarie.lenton58@gmail.com*

# My Story

*The names in this story have been changed to protect the identity of those involved.*

It was a pleasant birthday lunch with my wife and my stepmother when, to my surprise, my daughter Lisa arrived. Initially, I was quite amazed and pleased that she had remembered my birthday, but she walked up to the table and announced that my son was dead. We all looked at her in disbelief. We had been with him the previous night at his birthday party, arranged by him.

We really thought it was a joke, or a mistake. It could not be, but we questioned her. Obviously, we all thought it must have been a car accident. Then she told us: it was suicide. We were too stunned to comprehend what she said. It was only a few hours since we were all with him — with all his friends and family — and he was his usual happy self. He had even made some plans to go out with people, including to meet up with his stepsister the next Saturday.

Lisa told us that everyone had left the party, and those who lived at the house went to bed at about 2am. They left Steven in the lounge, listening to his favourite music.

When Lisa got up in the morning, she couldn't find the vacuum cleaner hose to start the big after-party clean-up, and Steven had gone out.

Then the police arrived and told them that a couple walking their dog early in the morning at a lookout area in the grounds of the large cemetery had found a young man in a car with a vacuum cleaner hose reaching from the exhaust to the inside of the car. The petrol had run out and the music CD had stopped. They called the police, but the young man was dead, and the details on the licence had led them to the address. They believed it was Steven.

Well, my birthday lunch was left, mainly uneaten. We went around to the house where Steven had lived with his brothers and sister. I asked my ex-wife if he had left a note of explanation, but was told that the note just said, "Take care of Jack (Steven's wee dog). He was the only one that cared." If he saw the number of people who attended his funeral (the largest one I've ever been to), then he would have realised that many, many people cared about him. Lots of young girls came up to me crying and needing comforting. Steven was a good-looking, fun-loving 28-year-old, with lots of gorgeous girls wanting to go out with him.

The days following and dealing with the funeral, were all a fog. We had to tell many family members and friends, and everyone always asked: "Why?" Well, we didn't know the answer to that, but talked over and over, trying to fathom out the reason. No matter how much we talked, we could not come up with a definitive cause.

We decided there may have been one reason, or an accumulation of reasons, that put together seemed insurmountable and led him to this irreversible point. Initially we were very angry with him to have done this, so selfish an act, from which there was no return. When we saw him at the funeral parlour, we asked him why, why? But it was too late for him to answer us.

I was told by my estranged wife that he had been on Prozac medication. I had not known about that, and was upset that I had never understood he was having any problems and needed help to get through them. He appeared to be perfectly happy in his life and

I was delighted that he had recently been offered a chance to be a partner in his boss's business. A great opportunity.

My new wife and I discussed why he had been so lacking in self-confidence that he couldn't face the future. We could see there may have been issues that could have led to his lack of confidence or depression.

Was it the ongoing pain and disability caused by a severe injury about twelve months before? Did this worry him that he wouldn't be able to continue in his job, because his leg and thigh were mangled and probably would be painful as he got older?

Or was his depression, which I was only just learning about, due to problems when he was born? Our first child was exceptionally bright, also blonde, blue-eyed and perfect. When my ex-wife had Steven, he was not the little girl she had looked forward to, and as a baby, he resembled a little monkey. She may have suffered from post-natal depression because I would come home from work to find her sitting still, ignoring the new little baby while he cried and cried. She just couldn't love him. I feel I was part of the problem at the beginning, too. I'd had a rough upbringing with very dysfunctional parents, so I was determined to provide well for my family, but unfortunately my job took me away from home a lot. When I returned, I worked especially hard to be a good, interactive father.

When the two little boys went to school, our elder son did brilliantly. Unfortunately, not understanding at that point about dyslexia, Steven was deemed a 'slow learner'. So, for years Steven struggled and must have felt inferior to his brother going through the school system ahead of him. He could never do as well but was always compared.

We tried all sorts of help for him. We found he was colour-blind, and his ambition had been to be a pilot. That was another disappointment. When he was fourteen, we contacted SPELD and I would take him to a helpful woman every Friday. She suggested he was dyslexic, and after talking to me and asking me to read a story, she decided that I was also dyslexic. She asked about my successes, and how had I managed to achieve them all? I told her that I surrounded myself by others who could take over the tasks that I couldn't do.

Did it bother him that he wouldn't be able to cope with bookwork in the offered partnership? If he had just discussed his worries with me, I could have steered him towards solutions. We knew he was a great leader of people and really appreciated by his fellow-workers.

I would have told him about really successful people who are also dyslexic but have overcome their difficulties, like Richard Branson.

For many years, Steven had a special girlfriend. They broke up and she moved on to get married, but Steven always held a torch for her. The music on the CD was their special song, and the spot where he chose to end his life was where they spent a lot of time together. I put a photo of his long-time love under his shirt, close to his heart, while I leant over his cold body.

When I attended the Coroner's Inquest, the coroner was quite scathing about the use of Prozac and how often he had seen suicides as a result of this drug. That made me sadder that Steven had not been able to talk about his depression, and instead went to his doctor for a magic cure. I had already realized that the GP involved was absolutely incompetent, and I had moved to another doctor.

At the inquest, a report was read out, which covered a subject that my ex-wife had revealed to me when we were organising Steven's funeral. Apparently, when his adopted sister Lisa was about twelve or thirteen, a teacher had asked the class if any of them had experienced child molestation. Lisa had put up her hand. There was an enquiry from the school – which I was completely unaware of as my ex-wife had instigated a separation and had completely hidden this drama from me.

It was reported at the inquest that Lisa told the school enquiry that she had been molested by Steven. The way she described it, it was MOST unlikely that it could have happened. Both my ex-wife and I agreed that it was a fabrication.

The coroner's report said that Lisa (then aged about twenty-two) had been telling Steven's friends about his abuse of her.

It was difficult for Steven to defend himself to his friends. Was this a contributing factor to him not being able to face carrying on?

Unfortunately, it soon became obvious that Lisa has a mental disorder. She had been adopted, and at the time, we did not know that this beautiful little girl's mother had an ongoing mental problem, inherited from her own mother. Lisa has been adamant that the sexual abuse occurred. But did it? Or was it a figment of her skewed imagination? Steven cannot help us with answers. He has gone.

Most of the family have totally disowned Lisa because they believe she caused Steven's death. She was always a game-player between the two younger brothers.

Our anger at Steven is that we will never have answers, or the opportunity to help him with whatever was bothering him. We cannot ask Lisa for 'the truth', because, as her stepsister says, Lisa believes her own truth; but is it really what happened?

Instead of trying to decide if Lisa is correct, and if Steven was at fault, we need to put all of that to one side and support the one person who is still alive – Lisa. Some of the family feel that continuing to help Lisa through her episodes means that we accept her story and therefore blame Steven for what she says happened. We don't. We are just trying to be non-judgemental, and help her in her own difficult life.

For many years after his death, I refused to acknowledge my birthday on April 13th. I was sad that Steven did what he did on my birthday. Some people asked if the date was deliberately chosen, but I don't think so. He listened to the one piece of music over and over and just didn't want to carry on.

I occasionally suffer from depression myself, mainly from injury pain, but the one thing he has taught me is that I would never contemplate suicide because I know the pain that it causes the people left behind. If he had died by accident, I think it would have been easier to bear, but he made this choice!

Every day I think of what this lovely young man has thrown away and will never experience. He would have been a great husband and father, and there were so many years ahead of him that he wasted. When I look at all my existing children and grandchildren, happy in their lives, it really breaks my heart.

Steven, you didn't think about what you were causing. It was so selfish. Why didn't you talk to us first? Given us a chance to change whatever was so bad. So many people loved you, but obviously you couldn't see that. You have left behind a family driven apart.

We all have our memories of time with you. Photos. Videos. But you are seldom spoken of between the family members, for fear of stirring up questions that can never be answered.

Steven's sudden death has been the most traumatic event that our family has ever suffered and over the twenty-plus years; the wound healed, but the scar will always be there.

To me, life is a wonderful and precious thing, and I try living every day to the full.

# What's Your Superpower?
Jess Sermak

I desperately wanted the autopsy report to come back with "cause of death: murder." I didn't want to feel as though she left me by choice... but, as I sat there at the work fax machine watching each page of the autopsy report spit out like it was just another case I was working on, I could feel my chest tighten and stomach churn. I wanted him to stay in gaol, I wanted him to rot in hell, I wanted it to just be all his fault! I wanted this nightmare to be over!

I watched as the last page escaped the fax machine, snatching it out and then running quickly into my office, shutting the door behind me. As a lawyer, this wasn't the first autopsy report I'd read; in fact, I'd probably read twenty before this one, but it was most definitely the hardest. It was the autopsy report of one of my greatest loves. The soul who gifted me life. The one who comforted me when I saw dark creatures in my nightmares. The person who held me as I wept, and questioned my self-worth when my first love broke up with me. The nurturing woman who would caress me and reassure me that everything would work out... that it would all be ok. Exactly what I knew I needed in this moment... but she was gone, and had been for the past nine months. Now, I was here, holding the final piece of this nightmare in my hands. I finally had the answers to the questions that had me lying awake every night since she died.

I felt the papers slip from my hands as tears began to cascade down my cheeks like waterfalls. I fell out of my chair and found myself instinctively curled in a ball under my desk, begging for someone, anyone, to take the pain away. It was now clear she was still alive, but unconscious, when he attacked her on three separate occasions. As he repeatedly whacked her with a fibreglass rod; she was still alive. As he hit her countless times in the face with a coffee mug, leaving multiple ceramic pieces in her face; she was still alive. As he punched and hit her all over her body; she was still alive.

However, no-one could prepare me for the final piece of my grief, the piece that left me questioning whether she truly loved me. The actual cause of death was finally revealed – asphyxiation. She had choked on her own vomit from the tablets she had ingested. She had committed suicide...

She had chosen to leave me and my three younger siblings, she had decided not to watch us grow up get married and have our own babies; instead, she chose death. Here I was, just twenty-four and fresh out of law school, back from a volunteering holiday in East Africa; I had my whole life ahead of me. My brothers and sister were just twenty-two, twenty and eighteen. Our lives would no longer include her; she was suddenly erased from all of our future memories.

I'm not sure I ever really expected her to die from suicide at her age, but sadly, suicide doesn't discriminate, and I've been forever changed by suicide in more ways than anyone ever should. Six months after my mother's suicide, my childhood friend took his own life too, he was just twenty years old... I was absolutely devastated. I had known him my whole life, our fathers were best friends. He was adventurous and fun, and would always have us kids on the floor laughing hysterically at his mischievous antics. I still miss him. I also grew up knowing that my grandmother on my father's side had committed suicide in 1986. I never really knew her, but I know she touched my mother's life deeply, as she was the last one to speak to her alive. And finally, suicide had touched my best friend. Too many failed attempts to count; the last time, she believes my mother curbed her attempt by somehow pushing her out of the bed.

But perhaps the most intimate relationship I've had with suicide was coming face to face with *him* myself. Challenging him – staring him straight into his piercing black yet alluring eyes. When I finally pried myself off the floor under my desk after reading her autopsy report, I decided in that moment that I would go home and end the excruciating pain I was in. It was finally time to fulfil what I believed was my destiny – to follow in my grandmother's footsteps, now my mother's footsteps, and kill myself. I was no longer afraid of death, I was numb. There was no hope left in me, and I couldn't see a way out of this deep dark hole that I was in. I couldn't see any light in the fog that surrounded me.

The strength and drive that I once had, had been engulfed by the pain of her death. Absorbed by the painful memories. The memory of walking into that dark, cold room with crimson curtains, towards a small white coffin in the middle of the room. Gathering the courage to peer into the coffin and, like a cold slap in the face, suddenly realising that there was no waking up from this nightmare; it was her... I felt my body buckle, tears exploding from my eyes, dripping onto her lifeless body. I found myself apologising again and again for not being there for her in her final hours, for not protecting her from him as he beat her, for letting her die alone, but mostly for not knowing how to save her from herself. I wanted to pick her up out of that coffin and hold her tight, reassuring her that everything was going to be ok. I was here now; no-one was going to hurt her again. Finally, I leaned into the coffin to say one last goodbye to her physical being, gently kissing her on the forehead and telling her how much I loved her. How she had made my life so wonderful! Our great love story had come to a tragic end.

My mother was the epitome of love, beautiful beyond words, and she always chose kindness. Despite having a horrific childhood, she loved hard and had a strong moral compass. She was such an old soul who was prophetically wise, and never judged people. She taught me that you never know where that soul has been, what they have had to endure, or what crimes may have been perpetrated against them. She was the reason I was who I was today!

People often ask me if I'm angry with my mother for what she did, and the simple answer is no. She had an illness. She struggled with depression and mental health issues for as long as I can remember. Even now, I tense up a little when I recall her on a bad day. Now, I understand that depression and anxiety are just like any other illness that needs to be properly diagnosed, treated and managed. However, back in the '80s and '90s, instead of getting the treatment she needed, she was often called crazy, psycho, unstable, and threatened with being committed against her will. It was such a taboo topic, and the stigma associated with it was terrible.

Perhaps if she had received the treatment and help that she needed she would still be alive today, sharing my life with me and my siblings. I thought that people were more understanding of it these days, but that hasn't always been the case. Whenever my mother's death comes up in conversation, I'm inevitably asked how she died... the look on their faces when I tell them she committed suicide is exactly the same whether they're nineteen or ninety. They expect me to say her death was the result of cancer or a tragic car accident. Instead, they don't quite know what to say after that. Often looking at me like, "Why, what did you do?" Or "Why didn't you get her the help she needed?" Sadly, the World Health Organisation estimates that one person every forty seconds commits suicide around the world, so why is there still this stigma? Why is more not being done about it?

I believe its derived from Christianity; coming from a Christian upbringing myself, many Christians believe that if someone commits suicide then they don't enter the gates of heaven. I will never forget the way my little sister looked up at me as we sat in the front row at my mother's funeral, holding each other up for support. We listened as the Pastor spoke about death and then, out of nowhere, insinuated that our beautiful, compassionate mummy would not get to meet her Jesus in Heaven. I didn't understand it; she was a devout Christian, a lover of Jesus who read her Bible every single day. For Christ's sake, we were even burying her *with* her beloved Bible. I couldn't understand how God can forgive you your sins, but if you committed suicide you would go to hell.

As those words left his mouth I watched as my twenty-year-old baby sister's gorgeous green eyes gazed into mine. Then suddenly they flooded with tears as she looked to me for confirmation that what he was saying wasn't true. I couldn't understand why he felt it was his place to say this as he stood before four young grieving children who had just lost their mum, and in front of all their friends and family. Unfortunately, it wasn't the only funeral I attended that year where it was inferred that the person in the coffin wasn't going to heaven because they, too, committed suicide. As a spiritual being, I know this is not true; their souls most certainly move forward on their spiritual journey!

*Battling Suicide*

After enduring nine months without her, instead of giving birth, I was desperate to die. I was so tired of being strong for everyone else that I didn't have any strength left in me to fight for my own life. I needed to feel her squeeze me tight, stroke my hair and tell me to rest, that it would all be ok, just like she would when I was a little girl. I wanted to end it so that I could finally be with her again, to feel her, to talk to her and to tell her how painful it had been without her by my side. To ask all of the questions that swirled around in my head night after night as I tried to sleep – what happened? Did she regret it? Why did she do it? Why did she choose to leave me? Why wasn't I enough for her to stay?

Something greater than myself stopped me from taking my own life that September afternoon. Whether it was God or the Universe, my mother, or my own spirit team, I'm so grateful that they did. Reflecting back, if I had ended my life that day, my soul would have missed out on so many incredible opportunities for growth and advancements. Two months after I stood face to face with suicide, I was surprised to discover I was pregnant with my beautiful son Joshyua! Joshyua has filled my life with so much joy and unconditional love that I've never come that close again to attempting suicide.

To think I could have missed out on the joy of being someone's mother if I decided to go through with it makes me very emotional. I have gone on to have such a wonderful life! I've stood in front of the man of my dreams and said yes to being his wife, I've given birth to two more incredible little souls, a girl and a boy, and I've been a foster carer to two beautiful little girls for the past three years.

My eyes have been graced with such beauty as I've travelled around the world. I've felt intense joy as I've skied down the slopes laughing with my brothers and sister in New Zealand, watched turtles hatch on Lady Elliot Island, swam in the gorgeous blue lagoon in Vanuatu, watched the sun set over Maui with my dad, and saw the moon rise whilst camping with all my kids. I've written a book, touched lives, bought a house, and coached women from all around the world! I've learnt to meditate, connect with my spirit team, and sit in the stillness.

Even though it's been almost twelve years since the police knocked on my door and told me she was deceased, I still miss her every single day! The pain has subsided because I know her spirit lives on. There are days when I will be doing something and will be reminded of her, or a certain smell will bring back a memory, and I feel that pain again. But instead of feeding into that pain, instead I like to think that she's thinking of me, too, in that moment – sending me a gentle reminder that she's still a part of my life. And if I ever feel like I start to forget her, all I have to do is look in the mirror and I see her in me. I know she lives on through me... she lives on through my children.

Despite being forever changed by multiple suicides, the greatest lesson suicide has gifted me is to know I'm enough just the way I am – to be authentically me! I would not be the woman I am today without the lessons those suicides, and my own attempt, taught me. As my dear friend Rhonda Ohlson always says, it's up to you to choose to turn your pain into your power. That power has fuelled my desire to become a Life Coach passionate about empowering women to be authentically themselves; to shift into their purpose and reclaim their own power. To help them learn how to re-align their lives and awaken again after tragedy. Even though I couldn't save my beloved mum, or my grandmother or my childhood friend, their stories give me the motivation and purpose to help women transform their own lives and create the life of their dreams – which gives each of them purpose even after their deaths.

Finally, I would like to leave you here with the reassurance that you are a divine gift. You are enough, right where you are in your life right now, and you are so incredibly worthy. Your uniqueness is your gift, and your story is waiting to be shared with others. It's now up to you, whether you turn that pain into your superpower or allow it to control the rest of your life...

Sending so much love, healing and blessings your way during this difficult time, my friend! xX

*If you wish to connect with Jess, you can contact her via her email: jessica.c.sword@gmail.com*

# Yellow Roses
## Tania Allen

Losing someone you care about and love is always difficult. However, when someone you love takes their own life, the haunting memories and feelings never leave you; they simply shift in intensity over time. Contrary to the opinions of others that you just need to get over it, this is not something you just get over. It is something you learn to live with and manage in your own unique and individual way. There is always the constant wondering of why and wishing you had seen the signs, wishing you had done more.

There is no predictable and defined timeline for healing and moving through grief, and there is no single right way to cope. Furthermore, the quick tips found on websites of how to cope after losing someone to suicide – although they mean well and sound quite straightforward on paper, reality says they couldn't be further from the real, raw, and often very painful journey that this overwhelming grief may take you on.

I hope that as you read my story, you find some hope and a little ray of sunshine, and know that it's okay to feel the feelings you feel at any given moment. It is also my intention that as you walk on the path to healing that you find some comfort in knowing you're not alone, and a level of certainty that you will move through the guilt, the feelings of deep, deep pain, and get back on the path to a better place. A place where the pain isn't so painful, the grief isn't so crippling, and the memories of your loved ones are beautiful memories that you will cherish always from a place of peace and love rather than a place of despair, sadness and loss.

## The mysterious man in the photograph

I will never forget the day I met the man that would leave a long-lasting impression on me. I was eighteen, and he was a photograph pinned up on the front door of a mate's house. It was December 30th, 1988. We were celebrating the end of the year. Who was this mysterious man in the photograph?

This mysterious man was Simon Daniel David Allen. A happy-go-lucky man with a great sense of humour. It sounds a little crazy, but I knew the moment I met him I was going to marry him. He was the life of the party, someone who would go out of his way to help others, whether family, friends, or complete strangers. He was a quiet man, a true down-to-earth gentleman. He wasn't perfect by any means. He had a temper that would appear every now and then; maybe only a few times a year, but when he burst, he burst. But all that was overridden by the genuinely good-hearted and -spirited man Simon was.

Simon had a vision to become something of himself and build something together for our family and our future. He had an eye for perfection and doing things right and doing the right thing. This was a man who was often insistent on holding my hand and skipping on a footpath of a main road with not a care in the world. Just happy in the moment. This was a man who would bring me yellow roses for no reason, simply just because he wanted to. So, what happened? What led to him making the decision to take his own life? It's a question that I will never be able to answer. There was no note, there was no goodbye, and now I return those yellow roses to his grave in loving memory of the beautiful man he was.

## Before the tragic ending to a beautiful man's life

We were married in 1991, and in the early days we found ourselves juggling a few jobs and starting a new business. It was fun and exciting as we embarked on building the foundations for our future. The business took off, and our busyness was fuelled with passion to build a future and provide an exceptional service to others. Simon's commitment to excellence was seen everywhere. He took absolute pride in everything. His garden was his sanctuary, and his love of critters and reptiles, and willingness to just go the extra mile for a complete stranger, was extraordinary.

By 1993, we were building our first house together. In 1996, we were welcoming our son Josh into the world with a fast-paced, rapidly expanding business. By 1998, we were starting another new chapter with the purchase of 5 acres in Sydney's north-west, and a vision to build our dream home. That same year, we were absolutely delighted when our baby girl Siobhan was born. Josh was Simon's little shadow, and Siobhan his precious little sweet pea.

Pressure was mounting, but nothing that didn't seem normal. Life was moving at a very fast pace; we employed many, had a thriving and very time-demanding business, enjoyed the company of many friends, and life was pretty good. Well, so I thought. A few cracks had started to appear, although some felt like they were big earthquakes. I never thought they would ever be a sign, or be part of the pieces of the puzzle that lead to his suicide.

## The knock at the door that changed my life

I remember the moment like it was yesterday. I heard a knock on the door. It was 6:24am, Monday the 26th of July 1999. I had been up a couple hours earlier with Simon attending to our recently born baby girl. Simon suggested I go back to bed whilst he fed her and settled her back down. That was not unusual, as he was a hands-on dad.

I must have fallen back to sleep, as the next thing I remember was a knock at my door.

Who was standing at the door is a bit of a blur. What isn't a blur, something I cannot erase from my memory, are words that no-one ever wants to hear.

"Simon's hanged himself, Tania."

My instant response was, "Is he dead?" The thoughts that rushed through my head at the speed of light were overwhelming. The hours that followed felt like I was in a movie. Functioning in a detached autopilot mode, there was no time to start grieving, no time to just stop for a moment and curl up and cry. There were the phone calls I had to make, the screams of disbelief down the phone. I'm not sure in what particular order the next sequence of events occurred. They just all seem to blend in together, and it all seemed to happen at once.

The question of why was at the forefront. What was said during his last phone call received by a builder just 30 minutes before he died? Did this tip him over the edge? Was he thinking about it the night before? Did the documentary we watched the night before, of the Hanging of Ned Kelly, put ideas into his head? Was it the pressures he had at the time from his father, or the business, or even me? Had this been building over time? What was it, and why? All these questions were spinning around so fast in my head without bringing me closer to one definite answer.

What broke my heart the most was telling my three-year-old Josh that Daddy was never coming back, and knowing that my ten-month-old baby girl would never have the chance to say "Daddy, I love you." What will our future hold? What happens now? These were thoughts that were rapid firing through my brain as I dealt with the other realities that demanded my time and attention when all I wanted to do is curl up on my bed. I was numb.

## Hindsight is a bitch.

Not all things are a "sign", or are they? When you lose someone to suicide, the first questions someone will ask you is "Why?" or "Did you not see any signs?" To be honest, it frustrates the heck out of me. I've often thought hindsight is a bitch. A contributor to guilt, sadness and regret. Why do things become so clear *after* the fact? Why is it in hindsight things are so obvious, when they weren't so clear at the time? On the flip side, just because we look back and see a BFO (a blinding flash of the obvious) doesn't mean that it was a sign. Perhaps it was nothing more than a normal reaction or response to everyday life. Not all things lead to suicide and not all things are a "sign".

Rather than offering comfort, hindsight often sends you down a deep dark rabbit warren of "what if" and "I should have done this" or "I could have done that". Sound familiar?

## Quick Tip: Looking back offers no opportunity to move forward

To stay on the path to healing and finding happiness and purpose, you must look forward. It's okay to look back with fond memories, but when you catch yourself looking back in regret or in a place of guilt or sadness and reflecting on what you could have done or should have done, it's important to shift quickly so you don't stay stuck for too long.

## Stigma and Judgement

Sadly, there is still to this day a horrific level of stigma around suicide. In the early days, I often found myself isolated and alone. The target of gossip and community whispers. Even as the years went on, my children felt isolated and alone often in the middle of judgement and whispers from so-called peers at school, all fuelled by the judgement from their parents. Friends disappeared out of my life as they couldn't cope, or didn't know how to have conversations about what had happened. Others asked me what sort of wife I was for my husband to commit suicide. It was horrible. Don't get me wrong, many people were very supportive, and the ones who stood by us I am forever grateful for. I found myself navigating my way through uncharted and very lonely waters for days, weeks, months, years, and decades after.

Society can be cruel, and people are ignorant. So be sure you've got your armour ready. I coped as I had plenty of armour to protect me and many masks I wore on different days. The "I'm coping" mask, the "business mode" mask, the "happy mummy" mask, and even the "everything is going to be fine" mask. Don't keep the masks on for too long though, as they can hold you back from releasing the pain buried deep inside.

Thank goodness mental health and suicide is widely spoken about these days; however, I still feel society has a long way to go before we see a world of deep compassion for the ones who take their life and the ones who are left behind, instead of shame, stigma and judgement. It's hard enough dealing with the loss of a loved one who has died by suicide, let alone having to deal with the gossip and judgement and shame that is so quickly placed on us for no reason from the thoughtless and often heartless people who, at the end of the day, don't even really care.

So, how do you get through this?

**Be Brave and Be Bold:**

Brave enough and bold enough to talk openly about mental health and suicide. By being open and honest about what you and your loved one has gone through, it kickstarts your path to healing and finding peace within your heart. It also opens the doors to conversation among communities, rather than keeping it locked behind closed doors. It's real, and it affects millions of people around the globe.

**Healing and finding peace**

Words like "You need to move on" are just devastating to someone who has lost a loved one, no matter how they die. I was a twenty-eight-year-old widow with a baby and a toddler and was told constantly that I needed to move on. I forced myself into dating again, and even remarried only a few years later. That second marriage lasted fifty-seven days, so I rest my case. You can't just move on. It doesn't work that way. Everyone goes through their own grieving and healing process in their own time and in their own way.

You may cycle in and out of the stages of grief in a backwards and upside-down order. Losing someone to suicide can trigger very intense emotions. Some of the emotions below may occur when you least expect it. These emotions might be triggered by certain events or non-events. There's no predictability as to when they will appear. Just like a rollercoaster, at times you will feel like you're being tossed around, up and down, and may find yourself screaming to get off. All I can say is hold on, as that time will pass, and the rollercoaster ride will eventually become easier.

Here's my quick tips on how to move through some of the real and raw emotions you may experience:

- **Shock.** Disbelief and emotional numbness are real and it's okay. It's a way for your body to cope. Reach out to people you love or professional support at this time.
- **Anger.** It's okay to be angry, and it's also okay not to be angry. You may direct your anger towards your loved one for abandoning you, or it may come out in other ways. It took me ten years to get angry at Simon for doing what he did. Yet, looking back, my anger came out in other ways. I was abrupt and intolerant to those who didn't seem to meet my expectations.
- **Guilt.** This one can destroy you if you allow it to. Replaying "what if" and "if only" scenarios in your mind won't bring your loved one back. Please know this is not your fault, and staying in guilt won't help you heal and shift into a higher, happier energy.
- **Despair.** Deep sadness, loneliness or helplessness is normal at some stage through the grieving and healing cycle. Be kind to yourself. Get help when you need it, and stay connected to friends and family who are understanding and supportive. Disconnect from those who are disempowering and unsupportive.
- **Disbelief and Confusion.** Trying to understand why our loved one has taken his or her life will be a forever quest. It is common to have some unanswered questions. Meditation and mindfulness can help you move out of a place of why and into a place of acceptance.
- **Rejection.** Rejection can run deep and wide. My daughter throughout her teens felt rejected by her father, wondering why he chose to leave and didn't want to see his kids grow up. I went through times where I felt I must not have been good enough. My son doesn't really speak about it to this day. Just know on some level, at some time, it's normal to feel rejected, and again, the sooner you can acknowledge your loved one was not

rejecting you but rather rejecting themselves and rejecting life, the sooner you can reconnect with them on a higher spiritual level.

- **Fit your own mask first.** If you have ever flown in an aeroplane, you would have heard the air steward remind you to fit your own oxygen mask before helping others. I wish someone had told me to fit my own mask first, as I feel my own healing would have come sooner. I often had no choice as I had two babies to raise, however fitting your own mask first is making a commitment to you. Losing someone through suicide is traumatic, and the emotional wounds run very deep and the scars never fully disappear.

Here's a few ways you can fit your own mask first on your path to healing and finding peace:

- **Grieve in your own way.** There is no right or wrong here, do what's right for you. Friends and family may have certain expectations around how or how long you should be grieving. Block out the noise, and do this in your own time, at your own pace. Know that it's okay to make time for you.
- **Be prepared for the painful triggers.** The future will always be filled with anniversaries, birthdays, milestones, and even people who may simply remind you of your loved one. Being prepared means you won't fall as fast or crash as hard. This could be as simple as not filling your week or day up so much. Take time out for you, make it a habit to do some extra nice things for yourself. Whatever works for you.
- **Keep in touch.** Reach out to friends and family for support. It's so easy to withdraw, not wanting to be a burden on others. It's important though to make sure you keep in touch with the right

people. The ones that can listen and hold you when you need it, and empower you when you are ready.

- **Trust in yourself.** This one is a big one. We often fall into a cycle of listening too much to others instead of listening to our heart and soul. Trust in you. I must say though, it's a good idea not to make any big decisions in the first 12 months after losing your loved one.

- **Consider a support group or professional support.** This is something to consider, however the right group is also important. Speaking with others who are experiencing the same type of grief may help, or perhaps support may come from a professional who is familiar with grief associated with losing a loved one by suicide.

**A final note. My gift to you.**

A few years ago, I was introduced to an ancient Hawaiian practice for healing called Ho'oponopono. Ho'oponopono means to make (ho'o) right (pono) right (pono). You can use Ho'oponopono for many reasons. It helps you release negative feelings, opens your heart. It dissolves anger and bitterness, guilt and despair. It can be practiced by all religions; that's why I love it so much. Ho'oponopono consists of four simple steps:

- Step 1: Say I'M SORRY...
- Step 2: Say PLEASE FORGIVE ME...
- Step 3: Say THANK YOU...
- Step 4: Say I LOVE YOU...

Say it as often as you like, for as little as five minutes a day.

At the time of writing, it has been more than twenty-one years since Simon died. He was just thirty-two. What I know to be true is even the happiest of people can take their own life. There are often no signs at all, or they are hidden and disguised very well. How you deal with the worst parts of your life shape your character more than anything else. Further to that, if you can take your worst experience and make it your best, then life is always a gift. That gift can then be used to help others.

I hope you experience healing through forgiveness and acceptance, and you find peace in your heart.

I'm sorry. Please forgive me. Thank You. I love you.

In memory of Simon Daniel David Allen. 29.05.1967 – 26.07.1999

*If you wish to connect with Tania, you can contact her via her email: tania@visionalliance.com.au*

# Together, We Can All Make A Difference
Aldwyn Altuney

I was first touched by suicide when I was thirty-two years of age.

I was working as a Journalist/Sub-Editor at the Daily News in Tweed Heads, and received a phone call from a colleague who had heard my friend, Cassandra Maria Dalziel, had hung herself.

At first, I didn't believe it. I thought, "Of all people, Cassandra would never do that." She was the most outgoing person, had everything going for her – a loving family, boyfriend, her own house. She was smart, always smiling and joyful.

I had known her for a few years as the communications manager of the Gold Coast Airport – a position she had recently retired from.

After two more phone calls, sitting at my desk in the newsroom one sunny day on December 5th, 2006, it was confirmed that Cassandra had taken her own life. She was thirty-one years of age – due to turn thirty-two on December 25.

I was thirty-two at the time – we were both born the same year, 1974.

When the reality of the situation sank in, I was in absolute shock. I didn't want to believe it, and couldn't understand why Cassandra would do that to herself.

She had depression though, and I now understand how it happened on what I call "the roller-coaster of life".

About three hundred people showed up for Cassandra's funeral at Greenmount beach in Coolangatta for a beautiful and solemn service, where her ashes were released into the ocean. She had no idea how many people she impacted.

Since then, I have had three male friends also take their own lives before the age of forty-five.

In fact, in the past year, I have lost eight friends or family members – seven of them under the age of sixty. Statistics show that one third of the world's population die by age sixty-five.

Every time someone I know dies, it's a reminder about how fragile life is and how important it is to celebrate every precious moment in life.

I believe we are all here for a purpose, and if someone chooses to take their own life, that is their choice, and I believe it's important to respect that – as hard as it may be.

A friend once said to me: "Depression is anger turned inwards."

For years, my father told me that "Anger is danger." So, I suppressed my anger for many years, and when I saw events happening in society that angered me such as wars, violence or animal cruelty, I felt hopeless and helpless to do anything about it, and internalised my anger mostly.

I found a release as a child through playing table tennis, poetry, music and later, the media.

I have suffered from depression and self-harm for years, often feeling alone and like I didn't belong.

I was born in Sydney's northern beaches and grew up in a loving household where my beautiful European parents, Michael and Nelly, went above and beyond to ensure myself and my brother Nick had a great life.

I have Greek, Turkish and Ukrainian heritage, and all three countries were at war with each other, so I call myself the "love child" now!

As a first generation Australian, I was bullied at North Balgowlah public school from the age of six. Fellow students would pick on me about my name, the food I took to school, the clothes I wore. Anything they could pick on, they did.

As such, I grew up angry with the world and my parents, and started rebelling from a young age.

I was running away from home at age thirteen while, ironically, I was also the number one ranked Australian junior table tennis player. I would release my anger with the sport, and developed a killer forehand smash!

At age fifteen, after being fed up with my constant rebellion to his strict rules, my dad kicked me out of the home and said, "You're not my daughter anymore."

I moved into a crazy household in Manly with a drug-addicted drummer, who I began to date, his alcoholic mother and drug dealing sister. I began doing two part time jobs at around five dollars per hour to cover my rent of fifty dollars per week.

This was a complete party house with non-stop music and jamming until sunrise each morning. After six months of this, with my boyfriend lying to me and cheating on me, there came a turning point.

I remember The Pretenders record, *Don't Get Me Wrong* playing on the turntable, and seeing my best friend at the time making love to my boyfriend in our bed.

I was sixteen years of age, and started bawling my eyes out. I called my mum in tears and said, "I can't handle this anymore."

She said, "come home," which I did, and even though my dad wasn't happy about it, I ended up studying very hard with my brother.

I had gone from Dux of North Balgowlah Primary School to failing everything in Year 11, and changed schools to Forest High School for Year 12.

That was another turning point – changing my environment. I discovered that the grass is not always greener on the other side, and started to appreciate my parents and family so much more.

I ended up qualifying to do a Bachelor of Arts in Communication (Media) at the University of Canberra (UC) from 1992 to 1994.

While there, noticing a job going for editor of the university newspaper, Curio, I applied three times before I was accepted. I took the fortnightly publication from twenty-four pages to forty-eight pages, and had thirty contributors that I was co-ordinating.

I became the longest serving editor at the paper and loved the power of the media to affect change in the community.

I found the media a great way to share my voice on what I felt were injustices in the world and ways we could help make it a better place to live.

One of the first stories I wrote was an anti-duck shooting story with the headline "Go and Get Ducked!" I couldn't believe people were shooting ducks for fun and that it was legal in Australia.

I continued to write stories about issues that moved me in some way, including battery farming of chickens, female circumcision, and stories about the environment.

By the time I graduated from university, I received High Distinctions in my majors of TV Production and Photojournalism.

This was the start of what ended up being a lucrative career in the media, where I went on to work as a journalist on TV, in radio and print media across Australia and internationally.

Since then, I have interviewed stars including Charlie Sheen, Jewel, Vanilla Ice, Hugh Jackman, Russell Crowe, Cyndi Lauper, Debbie Harry (Blondie), Alby Mangels, Jimmy Barnes, Jimeoin and Mikey Robins, among others.

I worked as a Journalist at The Daily Mercury in Mackay, Coffs Harbour Advocate, Queensland Times in Ipswich, Satellite Newspapers in Brisbane, Rave and Time Off in Brisbane, the Gold Coast Bulletin and Sun Community Newspapers (where I was a Journalist/Sub-Editor for five years).

In 2005, I invested seven thousand dollars in my first personal development course in the Hunter Valley, NSW, and to this day, have invested more than five hundred thousand dollars on business and marketing courses, as well as many different modalities of personal development. This has been invaluable for my mental health, the growth of my business and myself.

I started my business AA Xpose Photography in 2002 on the Gold Coast after having a few small car accidents working late nights with a photography company in Brisbane.

At the time, I was working as a journalist at the Gold Coast Sun Newspapers. When I left my position at the Sun, the business evolved into AA Xpose Media, as people began requesting PR work (publicity), copywriting, video, graphic design, writing, editing and media training services.

I did my first media training workshops in 2003 and had repeated calls for more.

In 2014, I launched an online media training program called Mass Media Mastery, where I teach people how to gain free publicity.

I now have clients from all over Australia, the US, UK, Netherlands, South Africa and New Zealand. Most of them are small businesspeople, authors, speakers, etc. and many I have never met before in person. Such is the power of online marketing.

I help people who have a great message, product or service to share it with the masses through online and offline media so they can achieve fame, fortune, freedom and leave a legacy.

I have covered some amazing events including the HP International Circle of Excellence Convention, Harcourts and SWAP International Conventions, International Women's Day Festival, National Caterers Association annual awards, UDIA gala ball, Australian Institute of Fitness and National College of Business graduation nights, Gold Coast Business Excellence Awards, Entertainment of the Year Awards for Clubs in South Queensland, Indy Carnival of Colours, International Legends of League Corporate Golf Day, Gold Coast Airport Marathon, and Blues on Broadbeach Festival.

There is never a dull moment with what I do.

Nowadays, I also run How to Gain $1m Worth of Free Publicity global workshops for authors, speakers, small businesspeople and social entrepreneurs.

I have members of my Mass Media Mastery online media training program and membership site from all over Australia and several countries overseas now, including the Netherlands, US, UK and NZ.

Passionate about raising awareness, appreciation and respect for animals, I founded the world's first Animal Action Day in 2007.

I have since run fourteen annual events, raising millions of dollars' worth of free publicity for different animal charities each year.

Passionate about promoting more good news stories in the mass media to help decrease depression and suicide rates worldwide and lift people's spirits, I founded a Global Good News Day on August 8th, 2018, and the Global Good News Challenge in June 2020.

A regular meetup group I run offering marketing advice is called Mass Media Tribe, and I co-launched the charity meetup group The Gold Coast Business Laughter Club on August 30th, 2018, to lift people's spirits in business.

I have over five hundred videos on my Media Queen TV channel on YouTube and love interviewing people, emceeing, speaking and inspiring people to live amazing lives.

In our good news PR company, our 7-step Mass Media Mastery system is so effective that we *guarantee* clients gain media coverage if they follow the system. We run the only media company I know of that guarantees media exposure with our PR packages.

Our mission is to use the power of the media to change lives worldwide, lift spirits and encourage people to open their minds through truth and good news.

I am passionate about inspiring a positive world where people are optimistic, living their passions and excited about their lives. A world where people love what they do and are excited about living life to their full potential and making a difference to the world around them. A world where more positive stories are being reported on in the mass media than negative ones.

I believe more good news stories being shared – both in traditional media (TV, radio and print) and online media – will help decrease depression and suicide rates worldwide.

I am also passionate about inspiring action for the humane treatment of animals worldwide, and am an advocate for people having compassion for themselves and others. For people speaking their truth and choosing love over fear as they speak up for what they truly believe in.

My wish is for people to understand and appreciate the miracle they are as human beings. Just by being born, they have beaten about 1 billion other swimmers to the finish line! Every person is a miracle and has a unique gift and message to bring to the world. I aim to inspire people to recognise and appreciate their gifts, to speak up and speak out about what they are passionate about. For them to get that they can create a ripple effect of change by being courageous and speaking their truth honestly and with integrity.

I stand for people waking up as individuals and collaborating with other awake people in the community to affect positive change in the world, particularly in the areas of health, peace, sustainability and environmental protection.

"Be the change you want to see in the world," as Gandhi said.

And I say: "Together, we can all make a difference."

*If you wish to connect with Aldwyn, you can contact her via her email: aldwyn@aaxpose.com*

# Forever Changed by Suicide

Jennifer Marilyn

My personal experiences with suicide don't make sense to me as I reflect on them. There is a history of mental illness in my family, and after a rocky adolescent phase in my life, I found myself self-harming and attempting suicide. Therefore, my family are now forever changed by suicide through my failed attempts and broken promises. As a twenty-one-year-old, having lost a friend I once considered the sister I picked, I promised my family that I would never put them through the pain I felt at that time – I have attempted to break that promise, though. And now, in my thirties, I find myself revisiting the feelings and the emotional turmoil that I encountered in my teens as I navigate new adult experiences of workplace bullying and the loss of my personal power to recognize that *I am a good person*.

Rewinding to my teens, I rebelled; I drank, I smoked marijuana, I was sexually abused, I was unsafe, and I was desperate for the approval of my peers. I was bullied, I clashed with my mum trying to reign me in from people-pleasing the peers at school encouraging me to be their toy for their own entertainment, and I had no idea how to manage all the emotions that came with navigating everything that I was going through. It was a quick transition from cutting, pinching and punching myself, and banging my head on the concrete as I lay crying and looking up at the sky, to stealing alcohol and pharmaceutical drugs from home and attempting to end my life. I woke one morning after taking a number of pills and drinking stolen wine and cutting my wrists to find myself alive; I was responsible for caring for my siblings that day as my Mum was at work, but I was taken to the hospital where nurses stood at the end of my bed speaking loudly to each other. "Yep, that's the one, the attention seeker." I felt so humiliated and hated. I saw counsellors and bounced back out of the dark spaces, only to find myself there again on and off for years. Every time I felt so helpless that I felt suicide was the only way out, I would hear all of the negative things that had been said to me over the years. From the nurses ridiculing me, to being told that being molested by a family friend was my fault because of how I dressed – it all came back into my head, compounding the sadness and self-loathing that I was already feeling.

When I reached my late teens, I was very much into the party scene, and many a night out turned to a two-day bender while high at a random stranger's place. I would toy with the idea of jumping off the building balcony or out a window – especially the morning I found myself trapped in an apartment with four men who fed me more and more drugs until they got what they wanted out of me. I felt so much shame, so much guilt. Oh, the guilt after a night of poor decision-making while under the influence of whatever I could get my hands on. Throughout this phase of my life, I had my partying besties, but Kathy was always the one that, like me, was always ready for an after party, and we would end up in all kinds of situations. Then I met my future fiancé, and backed away from the drug and party scene.

After settling down with my new partner, Kathy would call and ask me to come out or get her drugs, and I would let her know I wasn't doing that anymore. Kathy would still text and ask, and I just started ignoring her messages. One day, while at home on my own getting ready for work, I got a call from Kathy's sister. Kathy had taken her life. She had been addicted to ice, and threatened it many times apparently, and now she was gone. I questioned if I had a role to answer for in her suicide; she had been like a sister to me and then I just gave up on her, ignoring her calls. I should have tried to catch up for lunch, I should have done this or that, but I couldn't go back in time.

Going through the pain of losing Kathy led to me telling my family that I would never again make an attempt to end my life; I promised that I would never put them through the immeasurable pain that Kathy's loved ones and I was experiencing.

Years later, my fiancé and I broke up, and I was heartbroken. I couldn't work; I applied for credit cards and maxed them out, I self-harmed, started taking drugs again and drowned myself in alcohol. And then one night, under the influence of alcohol, I sent all of my family a good-bye text and drove out to where I had been proposed to and again tried to end my life. I passed out drunk and awoke hours later to dread. I drove back towards home and turned my phone on to find text messages and voicemails from my family, pleading with me to come home or answer my phone. Facing my family after that was horrible.

Even though the experience I put my family through was terrible, I then got help; I took medication and saw a psychologist. The first psychologist wasn't great – telling me that my ex broke up with me because he was cheating, and that all men are cheaters – but the support of my friends and family helped me to get back on track.

A few years later I bumped into Lesley, an old friend, while out clubbing. We used to get in trouble together in high school, and it was so nice to reconnect with her, we even worked a stocktake together. Unfortunately, whenever she would call and want to catch up, I was busy, and we lost touch. Months later, I was speaking to a friend who was going to a funeral the next day – a few questions later, I realized the funeral was for Lesley. Again, I was inundated with the questions of what I could have done differently to ensure Lesley was still here, and my feelings, guilt, regret, knowing that I would have been there for her if she had told me that she needed me.

I am not sure how it happened, but I started taking drugs again, which led me to meet a boyfriend who conveniently always had speed or ecstasy on him. I was also taking Duramine for weight loss and had stopped my anxiety medication. Once again, when this relationship ended, I lost the plot – not because my heart was broken, but because I couldn't process all of the lies that he had been telling me. I went for a night out with a friend only days after the relationship ended, and bumped into said ex; I then drunk drove and crashed my car. I was able to drive my car home (after a time that I knew everyone would be at work) and, afraid to face the music of my mistakes, I hid away in my back yard and tried to take my life again (I lived on bushy acreage and was easily able to hide in long grass at the back of the property). I could hear my mother's voice desperately calling out to me (she had seen my car and the damage to it) as I sat there, trying my hardest to make cuts on my wrists deep enough to end my life. Eventually, exhausted, I came out of the long grass and went to face the mess I had created again. My mother took me to hospital, and I started speaking to a counsellor and taking my anxiety medication again. I am reminded everyday of this, as the cuts on my wrists that should have been stitched at the hospital have left scars up both of my arms.

I was looking at the newspaper one morning before work in 2009 when I saw a photo of a friend of mine exiting the courthouse. I read the attached story and discovered that there was a murder investigation surrounding her mum. I called my friend, and the funeral was that day. I drove to work, bawling my eyes out. I showed my boss the newspaper article and, while choking back tears, explained that I needed to go to the funeral. When asked if I could work either side of the funeral, I was in shock!

I managed to get the whole day off and attended Dawn's funeral. I learned that there was an investigation to see if Dawn was murdered or committed suicide – Dawn had intended to take her life, but the timing between her being missing and the attack on her before she was discovered on a houseboat wasn't adding up. I had previously spent time attending different churches with Dawn, trying to find one that felt like home. I'd spent hours chatting with her while waiting for her daughter (my friend) to get ready for our planned nights out. My heart ached for Dawn's children as I could not fathom losing my mum; my heart broke for my friends.

While looking at Facebook in 2013, I saw an odd post by one of my friends. Confused by the post, I attended my friend's home on my lunch break. Her beautiful partner Matt had hung himself in her/their backyard. This is the same guy that generously went out and bought jumper leads to jump start my car when it wouldn't start. The same guy that saw my name on a Coke bottle and had to buy it for me. The same guy that had mowed the lawns that weekend, and invited my friend's sister and her then-partner over for drinks the night he took his life, obviously planning for my friend to have someone there with her when he left this earth. My friend and her children were crushed, are still crushed. My friend bravely spoke at Matt's funeral; her strength then and still now is unbelievable. She never hated Matt for what he did, she understood that he needed the hurting to stop. She still loved him deeply.

Today, it is 2020. Every time I see another child has taken their life due to bullying, I want to scream. I know what it is like to be targeted, and I want to tell every person thinking of taking their life that there are always other options; but people are cruel, and when you are inside your own head and feeling helpless and hopeless, I know how it feels. I passionately want to stomp out bullying in schools and workplaces. I regret every mean word I said to my peers when I was at high school, as while I was bullied, I am also guilty of picking on some undeserving people, too.

Life is hard, mental health makes it harder. I am medicated, daily, and I don't care about the stigma around it, I know that the medication helps me think straight and not be irrational. Even though I am going through a rough patch at the moment and thoughts of suicide have entered my head again, I am working hard to push them away. I know people care about me and would drop everything to support me. I know I am loved; I know that I am a good person. I am seeing a psychologist while I work through this rough patch and have coping techniques that I am using. I know that it is a bad day/week/time, not a bad life.

After all of the ups and downs and experiences that I have had with suicide, too many to mention here, I am so glad that I now have a safety plan. I have spoken to my friends and family and have supports in place. It was hard to open up, but it was for the best; the responses from my friends (the four that I have told) have shown me that I am loved and supported, and that is enough for me to be strong enough to stay here and keep living this life. Likewise, I advocate strongly for anyone I know to come to me if they are in a dark place and need someone to listen/hug/spend time with, because I would rather be woken up at 3am and make an emergency drive to support someone than work through losing another person I loved to suicide.

If my story has resonated with anyone reading it, please know that it is okay to struggle. Reach out to people and have a safety plan, because the pain won't last forever and those that love you always wonder what they could have done differently when they are left behind. It's okay to not be okay. Mental health care plans are only a doctor's appointment away, and you can shop around for a counsellor or psychologist that you feel comfortable with. Opening up to people, I have found so many people take medication to manage their emotions, and there is nothing wrong with that. However, if you are placed on a medication that doesn't feel right, let your doctor know as there are many different options available. Please use what works for you to work through your emotions: journaling, writing, poetry, exercise, being in nature, sunlight, grounding to the earth, being in water, talking, or anything else that helps you work through what is hindering you. You can also forever change someone who is considering suicide by letting people know they can approach you. Always consider that your words can be a weapon, and carefully consider the ones that you use. Smile at strangers, say hello as you pass people by, be the change you want to see in the world.

May everyone reading this live in the happy moments.

Love, Jenny.

# Suicide Survivor

## Emily Strange

There was a violent war in my mind. A fight that that left me feeling battled and utterly broken many times. It completely baffled me how I ended up in this hellish place. I was so stuck within the depths of my darkest thoughts, where no light seemed to shine. The dreams of my daring self and sunshine of my soul were nowhere to be seen. The blue-eyed, small-town country girl who loved to surf and soak in the sea, so lost and far from home. Looking for myself in other people, places and things. Chasing validation from everyone around me, doubting whatever decisions I made. Deep rooted feelings of unworthiness and loneliness. I was so fearful of the future, and a prisoner of my painful past.

Depression and anxiety were not new to me. The dark places they could take me were familiar. Although I had already overcome a lot of adversities with my own mindset, I could never understand where all this pain and suffering I was feeling had come from. My childhood was great. I was a happy and bubbly little girl with a lot of family and friends who adore me. Growing up, I was bullied throughout high school and became very detached from my body. Years of education, yet nobody taught us how or why it is so important to love ourself. The burden of bulimia started controlling my life when I was seventeen. My self-esteem was at an all-time low. I went to extremes to change how I feel, paying ten thousand dollars for breast implants when I was nineteen because I truly believed I would not be enough with my small, natural breasts. What other people thought of me is how I felt about myself. I placed so much reliance on everyone and everything around me going the way I think it should. Experiencing the lowest of lows and highest of highs.

I did a lot of geographical changes too, thinking that my problems would magically disappear by moving to a different town. Eventually realising that this was not the case, I then started doing a lot of personal development, seeking professional support and immersing myself into the world of spirituality. I slowly began to see a light at the end of this very dark tunnel that I seemed to have been stuck in for years. My confidence grew, I removed my breast implants, and I started showing up as my authentic self. It was a glimpse of hope into what my life could be. However, being so sensitive, feeling everything so very deeply, I was still so unaware how to digest my emotions.

Beneath the surface of beautiful Broome, I was dangerously caught up in its heavy drinking culture when I moved there to live with my younger sister. My world had been flipped upside down after a recent relationship break up. My mental health was deteriorating rapidly. I could not see past the pain. My own thoughts taking me to a very dark and lonely place, a place I knew well, but this was a whole new level. The bottom of all rock bottoms. Drowning in my own sadness and sorrow. Saturated by self-loathing. Years of excruciating memories replaying over and over, ones that would not even seem alarming to other people but had left me feeling traumatised. Too ashamed to admit how much I was struggling because of this brutal stigma that hangs heavy over mental health, despite society trying to remove this. Not knowing how to get help in this small country town or who to talk to, I continued partying on weekends, attempting to numb the severity of this internal pain. I was drinking to get drunk. Feeling very fragile from the intoxicated nights and harsh hangovers. Suicidal thoughts filled my mind frequently, but I pushed them to the side each time and suffered in silence. I was fragile like a bomb, and it was only a matter of time before I would explode.

At twenty-three years young, on the 23rd of August 2019, the walls came crumbling down. Just like a soldier on a battlefield at the end of a losing war, my hands were up in the air. I had no fight left in me. Crawling through the shattering pieces of my broken heart, my tank was beyond empty and all hope was gone. Mentally, physically and spiritually defeated. The agony of my aching body, the sadness of my suffering soul and heaviness of my hurting heart were unbearable. It's not that I wanted to die, I desperately wanted to live. In that moment though, with the drunken state that my mind was in, there was no choice. It was time to end this pain.

Drinking alcohol, a lot of it, to try fit in and forget. Surrounded by a crowd of people, but it was like I didn't even exist. An emptiness begging to be filled, yet I couldn't understand how it felt so heavy. Somehow making it home at three am highly intoxicated, my vision was very blurry. My thoughts were impulsive and my hands shaking as I fumbled around in the kitchen in search of my car keys. My sister woke up, anxiously demanding me to stop, but there was no common sense in this situation, all logic had rapidly disappeared and there was nothing that could stop me. Driving in blackout to the beach, then recklessly swallowing all of my antidepressant medication. My racing heart was soon replaced with a calming sense of relief, knowing that this was about to be over. Freedom felt so close.

Running for what felt like hours across the cold, wet sand of Cable Beach in the early hours of the morning. The ocean lit up by the moonlight and the sound of the waves crashing against the shore soothed my fear-driven mind. I needed to hide so nobody would find me. That's the only thing that made sense. Run and hide. Finally finding a place to lie down, I collapsed against a sand dune and rested my head against the shrubs. Looking up to the night sky, keeping my focus on the moon. I pulled my knees into my chest and hugged them tight. Closing my eyes for what I thought would be the last time, I sobbed myself into a deep sleep.

Against all odds, against all logic, I survived. There I was, despite it all, still breathing. What must have been hours later, I was drifting in and out of consciousness as police and ambulance officers were shaking me convulsively, yelling, "Is she dead? Is she dead? Hello, can you hear us?" as they desperately tried to get a response. Unable to move or speak, I was there, but not there.

Briefly finding the strength to open my eyes and get a glimpse of my surroundings, I was very confused, so unsure as to what was happening. Stringing together pieces of last night's decisions, this was definitely not a dream. I was somehow still alive. It was only later that I would know this to be a miracle, but right then, I was in a real-life nightmare.

Bright lights were piercing my eyes as I came to the shocking discovery that I was now in an ambulance. It suddenly felt like I was a little girl again, so fearful for my life, and all my senses of security and safety were threatened. The ambulance officer must have picked up on this energy and the worried look on my face. She graciously grabbed my hand and reassuringly said, "You're safe now, sweetheart." The significant genuineness in her voice ignited a small amount of hope in me, even while I was in this distressed state. The kind of hope that made me believe that maybe one day, I would be okay again.

Waking up in hospital, my best friend on one side, I could feel that her hand was placed on top of mine and noticed tears rolling down her cheeks. My sister standing at the end of the bed, staring deeply into my soul, and the look on her face is one that I will never forget. My heart broke all over again, in a way that left me with the only one decision. I had to stop fighting. It was time to surrender. I had to become the hero of my own story and make some serious changes. Seeing the pain I had caused was devastating. If I wasn't doing this for me, I had to do it for them. It wasn't just my life that had turned to turmoil. Alcohol and my distorted decision-making were like a destructive cyclone, causing so much chaos in the lives of people that I love and care about.

Living in a country town, the word got around what had happened. There was very minimal support available and I was given no guidance leaving hospital. I felt extremely isolated. People who I considered as close friends stopped inviting me to things. Doctor's prescribed me with more medication that actually increased my suicidal thinking. I was just another number in the system. Left alone to fend for myself. Without the support of my beautiful mother, encouraging me every day, it would have been another disaster waiting to happen.

What came next was a slow re-building of the foundations of my life, putting back together the broken pieces of myself and starting to mend relationships that had been hurt. The decision to give up alcohol came easy, but staying sober didn't. Not even the consequences of that night stopped me from drinking again. After two months without it and finding peace from abstinence, I then turned to partying again, forgetting that removing alcohol was a huge factor as to why I was feeling better. It was my way of coping though, and I didn't have the awareness or confidence to know how to stop.

No journey of recovery and healing is going to a straight road, but eventually running away from my problems became more painful than facing them. One day at a time I started to put all of my belief into a life of freedom, love and happiness. I started working with a life coach to make empowering decisions, created vision boards to keep me focused, found a 12-step recovery program for alcohol, surrounded myself with people who lift me, immersed myself in nature and continued seeking professional support for my mindset.

Unfortunately, I felt that I wasn't going to get any better in Broome with the lack of resources available. I moved to Perth to start fresh. There needs to be drastic changes to our mental health system, especially in rural and regional country towns. Suicide statistics continue rising and mental illnesses are becoming increasingly common.

Telling every detail of my story is not necessary, but what I will tell you is that we are all capable of using our mind to thrive instead of just survive. I am living proof. We all have a choice and a decision to make. Whatever choice we make, that is our solution. Not all of us choose to stay, the pain is too much, and that is okay. That decision was made based on true feelings in that moment. We cannot blame those who did decide to leave, and we cannot beat ourselves up for not being able to stop that. Everyone has a battle to fight; often it is a tragic silent suffering. Those who are left behind, those who survived, we can choose to speak up. We can end the silence by sharing our story of hope.

*If you wish to connect with Emily, you can contact her via her email: emkstrange@gmail.com*

# From A Parent's Point of View
## Sharon Davies

This is my story of my son, Matthew.

This chapter is from my point of view of the challenges that I personally faced as a parent. Watching my son attempt suicide six times was horrific and as a parent you feel useless, and you can't change their thought patterns.

Sometimes you feel like it's a time bomb ticking, and it always happen when you least expect it.

As parents we love our children, we understand them with unconditional love, right? It's what we do.

However, when Matthew's attempts started to happen, he would say to me that he felt there was no purpose in life for him.

It was crushing to hear that; as a mum you become speechless as you just don't know what to say, what to do and who to go to for help.

Who prepares you for that, right?

I found that through each year that I experienced these attempts with Matthew, I did not know what to believe.

Each suicide attempted, Matthew just keeps getting closer and closer to death. I just did not understand why he was trying to kill himself, as we were starting to get help through counselling. At the hospital, Matthew would comment to me, "I promise, mum, I won't do it again."

As a parent, you have your guard up as you worry each time the phone rings and it's the hospital calling.

"Oh, here we go again, it's the hospital."

You get that pit in your stomach, your anxiety feelings go up, and you become numb.

It is one of the hardest things I have ever experienced in my life as a parent.

There is no rule book.

It is also hard for other siblings in the family to understand the emotions of what you, and they, are going through. As a parent you must stay even stronger.

Oh, and a piece of advice: don't listen to people that haven't been in your situation. They have no idea of the emotions you are going through. Take my advice on that one. So many times, I would receive other people's opinions on what I should be doing as a parent. Many times I cried, I prayed, and I screamed, "WHY US?"

This is our story.

Matthew is a beautiful person and has a heart gold, and would help anyone. He is shy, funny, cheeky, and you just cannot help but love him.

Matthew has borderline personality disorder, ADHD and other health issues.

He suffers with depression, and it is managed now.

Matthew's suicide attempts all started with him trying to fit into society after he finished year 12 in 2005. I was a single mum at the time, and I received a promotion to leave Brisbane and relocate to Melbourne as a sales manager in 2007.

There was no question – I wasn't leaving Matthew behind in Brisbane with his father and brother. He wanted to be with me, so we both moved to Melbourne. We thought exciting times and a new adventure would begin in Melbourne. I moved first, and Matthew followed six weeks later.

In Melbourne I have a support network of my personal family which would be nice for a change as they were just around the corner. I knew the move would be perfect for us both – but I was wrong.

Matthew decided he wanted to go to TAFE in Frankston to learn IT networking. I thought, okay, let's give it a go. With Matthew's disabilities, he would have support at TAFE. He would catch the bus and train and he was okay, and all was going well.

Until the day the bulling, gangs and harassment in the area started.

On his first attempt, Matthew swallowed a bottle of aspirin. My brother-in-law helped me to take Matthew to the hospital, as we were shocked at what happened.

Matthew explained that he was bashed, and the boys where going bash him again if they saw him. The hospital said it would be best for Matt to move back to Brisbane, which we organised after a long conversation with Matt's dad.

Matthew was now in serious depression. I still had another eight months left of my contract; I could not just leave Melbourne. But as soon as my contract was over, I was heading back for Matthew.

It was best that Matthew moved home, so he did. He was twenty by then.

Matthew did struggle living on his own in Brisbane while I was still in Melbourne. His depression was still not dealt with, but I thought he was okay. He was getting counselling, and was in a house with another boy and a care support. But they didn't see the signs.

I moved back to QLD and resided on the Gold Coast with my current husband. It's January 2010, it's pouring with rain, I had my family up from Melbourne, and it's starting to flood in Brisbane – a call comes from the Prince Charles hospital's mental health ward.

It's happening again. Second attempt at suicide, another bottle of tablets and sleeping pills. They got to him just in time. Off I go to the hospital to see Matthew and find out what happened and why.

After Matthew came out of hospital, I moved him to the Gold Coast so I could help him and find a better situation for accommodation.

It's now 2011; we find this perfect single unit under a house for Matthew in Southport, and he loves it. We take a twelve-month lease. Happy days for Matthew, and he is getting into a routine and has structure – shops and doctors just down the road.

Just when I thinks it's all good – NO. I get a call from the Gold Coast Hospital's mental health ward, and they tell me he doesn't belong here, and that I have to take him home.

In a six-month period, Matthew attended the Gold Coast mental health ward four more times, and the attempts were getting worse.

On the last one, I didn't think he would make it, as he had swallowed petrol and tablets and slashed his wrists. I thought he was gone. The smell of petrol on his breath and clothes and the blood on his arms was horrific. I don't think I will ever forget that situation. Oh, and all the doctors couldn't tell me if he would make it or not. And they don't know the long-term effects of what Matthew had done to himself.

He made it through the night.

By this stage, as a parent, I had no more tears. I was angry, numb, and I was ready to give up. Then I had a chat to one of the social workers that specialize in disabilities and mental health, and there was a light. I prayed so hard that Matthew would make it. How can you give up when you have brought this life into the world? I stopped crying and pulled myself together. When in doubt and I don't understand something, I research.

I started searching the net for help on the Gold Coast, and that is when I found the Mental Illness Fellowship Queensland (MFIQ). If it wasn't for my determination, I would never have found them and gotten support for Matthew. I helped MIFQ change the process in the hospital and the mental health ward for parents, as that was my way of dealing with Matthew's attempts and depressions.

Once Matthew finally got checked out of the Gold Coast mental health ward, he had to make a commitment that he would attend Ashmore Mental Health Clinic with a ten-week program to learn strategies to cope in the real world. And the good news is, he did – and if he made any attempts there would be three warnings, and he would get kicked off the program.

The doctor's and psychologist's support were amazing, and they also helped *me* to learn how to cope as a parent with the stress of Matthew's attempts; the biggest thing that I had to learn was not to be the rescuer or the victim. As a parent, there were lots of strategies to learn.

To this day, great news to share! Matthew has come through all of the dark days and dark places, and he has moved forward in such a big way. He wants to live and help others. He has just finished a Certification 3 in Aged Care, and wants to look after others. He has his own apartment and is living independently, with carers twice a week, a counsellor, and we have family dinner every Sunday.

Life is good, and as a parent, I am so grateful that I took the initiative to find the help from the people that can help my son. To this day I still keep my wits about me with Matthew, but I am aware of the signs to look for. I pray and I thank God that Matthew is still with us. He is now thirty-two.

God Bless. The End.

*If you wish to connect with Sharon, you can contact her via her email: sharon@sales2success.com.au*

# What Do We Really Know About Grief?
## Leesa Taylor

*There is life before grief ... and then there is life after grief. And somewhere in between, there is all-consuming grief. The death of a loved one is such a life-changing event, and yet an experience that often we know so little about. The funeral home may hand the newly bereaved a brochure explaining grief, and it may be read in the hope of finding answers to the many swirling questions: Am I going crazy? Am I grieving properly? How long will this last? When will I feel normal again? Should I be feeling like this? This may be the first glimpse of information about grief that the bereaved has ever read. Unless we have some professional reason to understand grief, we are not generally educated about it, but it is something that nearly all of us, at some stage, will have to experience. Some will be spared the experience until they are older, but some will experience it early in their lives, so often completely unprepared and left dazed by its intensity. And still others will experience it many times over. Some knowledge about grief is therefore important, not just for those that are going through it, but for support networks and society in general. This writing is offered as information only and not as professional advice.*

The grief experience is complex and multidimensional – to oversimplify it is to under-estimate it. Grief is not something that we simply recover from – it is something that we learn to live with, it becomes part of our story. Grief, like pain, is hard to unanimously describe, and what one person might feel and describe may be different to another's experience of the same event. Grief, until it has been part of a lived experience, is often a mystery. And even when going through it, grief unfolds itself in its own time and way.

To look forward, we can often look to the past to gain a sense of the now. Grief is no different. There are many theories relating to the grief process and how we adapt to loss. This in itself highlights that scholars are continually exploring the grief experience and how a person can be supported to adapt to loss. This chapter cannot do justice to all the theories, but will highlight four of the more well-known learnings that are relatable for many.

**Why is each person's grief story unique?**

To explain a little about the complexity of grief and why everyone has a different story to tell about their own experience, let's first look at the grief process as described in theories, then the grief reactions and factors that can contribute to making each experience unique.

**Staged Model of Grief**

One of the more well-known theories about how a person adapts to loss was developed by Kubler-Ross in 1969. This model was based on her clinical work with terminally ill patients. The model began with working through the denial of reality of the loss, then anger, bargaining, depression, before finally moving to acceptance and resolution. Failure to progress through the stages implied unfinished grief work and intervention needed[1]. This theory and other staged theories of grief have since been discarded by other scholars as a one-size-fits-all model that lacks acknowledgement of the unique reactions and factors of everyone's lived experience. This model has been suggested to be over simplified and does not take into account secondary stressors that a person may experience, as well as the social and cultural content of grieving[1,2].

## The four tasks of grieving

Another theory was developed by J.W. Worden in 1982, who adjusted it in years 1991, 2002 and 2009. Worden's task model suggested that grieving is an active process which requires the bereaved to take part in four tasks. The four tasks are not to be completed in any order or stages; they can be completed at the same time, individually, or even revisited. The first task is to accept the reality of the loss. This means not just acknowledging that the person has died, but emotionally acknowledging the loss. The second task is to process the pain. This requires embracing the feelings, acknowledging that it is appropriate to experience pain while grieving. The third is to adjust to the environment without the deceased in it. This might require the person take on new roles and responsibilities; not just taking on physical roles, but taking on a new way of seeing the world without the deceased in it. This task may take some time. The fourth task, which is the one that has been adjusted, is to find an enduring connection with the deceased in the midst of embarking on a new life. This does not mean forgetting the loved one, but finding a way of letting their memory live on, while also being able to embrace life with a reconceived personal identity[3].

## The Dual Process Model

Building on the strengths and perceived limitations of other grief models, Stroebe and Schut developed the "dual-process model"[4] in 1999. This process has three parts that a bereaved person will employ as part of the coping process. The first is described as the *"loss-orientated process"*[5(p277)]; this is where the bereaved person will concentrate on appraising and processing some aspects of the loss experience itself. This might include painful dwelling on the person they have lost, the event or searching for them in some way. The second part is *"restoration-orientation"*[5(p277)]; this focus is on stressors that are consequences of the loss, the struggle to reorientate life without the deceased person in it. The third element is *"oscillation"*[5(p278)] *between the two*. The underlying principle of oscillation identifies that a bereaved person will go back and forth between loss-orientation and restoration-orientation, necessary for adaptive coping. They may confront the loss and at other times avoid it; sometimes there will be periods when the person is not grieving at all, as grieving is often exhausting. As time goes on, a person may spend more time in one process than the other, and eventually, less time in both[5].

## Reconstruction of meaning

A post-modern social constructionist approach to coping with grief is more about *not breaking bonds,* but *constructing meaning out of the grief experience*. There have been various psychologists from the '90s to early 2000s who have developed this theory, including a well-respected professor called Robert Niemeyer Ph.D. The emphasis of the constructivist approach is on reconstruction of meaning or "meaning-making" in the bereaved person's life. It has been asserted that this process, in response to loss, is a central process in grieving – making meaning of the loss, especially when the death has been violent; or someone close to the bereaved person is considered particularly important[6].

## The grief response and the factors that make our story unique

Theories, formed from observations and learnings of human experiences, demonstrate the complexity and multidimensional nature of grief. Grief does not happen in isolation. So many other factors impact on each person's story, responses and unique experience of grief. Factors such as: an individual's **personal background** – the closeness or attachment to the person who has died, the person's age, culture, religious beliefs, gender and previous experience with loss, education level, time since the loss, and even the person's grieving style; the **Event** surrounding the death – was the death anticipated or sudden, traumatic, violent, painful or peaceful? Did the event trigger family issues or bring family together?; and lastly, **socio-environmental factors** – the social support system the person has around them, access to health care or professional support, the work environment, the sports or social groups the person belongs to, the neighbourhood or church group, or extended family network[7].

**The grief response** is something not openly spoken about enough, and as a result, is often not well understood when someone finds themselves in the midst of it! The response can include *psychological*, *physical* and *spiritual reactions*. "Grief, along with its associated thoughts, feelings, and behaviours, is one of the most powerful emotions that humans experience."[8(p401)] People will respond differently – some may display many of the recognised behaviours and physical reactions, whereas others may not display any.

Most people are familiar with some of the *psychological* and *behavioural reactions* often portrayed in films – crying, preoccupation with images of the deceased, social withdrawal, decreased concentration and attention, restlessness, anxiety, lack of appetite[9], guilt, anger, numbness, shock and a feeling of helplessness[10]. The *physical reactions* are less known; they can include suppression of the autoimmune system, sleep disruption, fatigue, muscle weakness, heart palpitations and chest pain, weight loss, headaches, muscle aches, nausea, menstrual irregularities, pain and sensitivity to noise[9]. Some of the health effects of grief are in response to the release of a stress hormone called cortisol. Cortisol levels may remain high for up to six months in people who have lost someone close. This can reduce the body's capacity to fight off infection and reduce inflammation; it may affect energy stores and prevent wound healing. This may also be the reason some people experience irregular heart rhythms and other associated heart problems[11]. *Spiritually,* the experience of grief can test a person's philosophical framework and assumptions about religion, life in general and about how the universe works. Some people experience post traumatic growth through their trauma of loss, revising a prior understanding of themselves and life, death and purpose[12].

**For You**

Grief is a personal, interwoven story. Comfort may be found in other's grief stories, validating a feeling, offering some hope where hope may have been lost, or providing reassurance that it is possible to have a life after loss. Finding a safe place and a way to tell your grief story, to express and acknowledge your thoughts and feelings is important and finding that place or way becomes a part of your journey and your story. I found my safe place in a self-help support group where I found people who were comfortable listening to and hearing my story, which I told over and over; each time it changed, and each time it helped me process the loss.

Be kind and gentle with yourself, name the feelings as they come in waves, know the waves will feel like they are pummelling you at first, but also know they will flatten out over time and instead of fighting the waves you will learn to lean into them and eventually ride them.

## Reference List:

1.  Meagher DK, Balk DE, eds. *Handbook of Thanatology*. 2nd ed. New York: Routledge; 2013.

2.  Stroebe M, Schut H, Boerner K. Cautioning Health-Care Professionals: Bereaved Persons Are Misguided Through the Stages of Grief. *Omega (United States)*. 2017;74(4):455-473.

3.  Worden JW. *Grief Counselling and Grief Therapy: A Handbook for the Mental Health Practitioner*. 4th ed. New York: Springer Publishing Company; 2009.

4.  Stroebe M, Schut H. The Dual Process Model of Coping with bereavement: Rationale and description. *J Public Adm Res Theory*. 1999;23:197-224.

5.  Stroebe M, Schut H. The dual process model of coping with bereavement: A decade on. *Omega J Death Dying*. 2010;61(4):273-289.

6.  Rozalski V, Holland JM, Neimeyer RA. Circumstances of Death and Complicated Grief: Indirect Associations Through Meaning Made of Loss. *J Loss Trauma*. 2017;22(1):11-23.

7.  Balk DE. Life Span Issues and Loss, Grief, and Mourning: Adulthood. In: Meagher DK, Balk DE, eds. *Handbook of Thanatology*. 2nd ed. New York; 2013.

8.  Rack JJ, Burleson BR, Bodie GD, Holmstrom AJ, Servaty-Seib H. Bereaved adults' evaluations of grief management messages: Effects of message person centeredness, recipient individual differences, and contextual factors. *Death Stud*. 2008;32(5):399-427.

9.  Doka KJ, Martin TL. *Grieving Beyond Gender: Understanding the Ways Men and Women Mourn*. Revised. New York: Routledge; 2010.

10. Stroebe M, Schut H, Stroebe W. Health outcomes of bereavement. [Norwegian]. [References]. *Lancet*.

2007;370:1960-1973.

11. Stamp N. *Can You Die of A Broken Heart*. Crows Nest: Murdoch Books Australia; 2018.

12. Davis C. Redefining goals and redefining self: A closer look at post traumatic growth following loss. In: Stroebe MS, Hansson R, Schut H, Stroebe W, eds. *Hanbook of Bereavement Research and Practice: Advances in Theory and Interventions*. Electronic. Washington DC: American Psychological Association, Inc; 2013.

*Leesa Taylor is a doctoral student who is studying thanatology (the field of death, dying and grief) and organisational behaviour. She has a lived experience of loss, with her husband suddenly passing away of heart failure. Three and a half years later she left her professional life to concentrate on the issue of how an organisation supports a bereaved employee. This chapter is a small glimpse into some of the evidence she has gathered to highlight how a bereaved employee is affected by grief and how the response from an organisation can either be supportive or contribute to the stress and trauma the employee is already enduring.*

# Resource List

<u>In Australia:</u>

❖ **Alcoholics Anonymous Australia:** 1300 222 222

❖ **Australian Government Dept of Health – Suicide Prevention:**

https://www.health.gov.au/health-topics/suicide-prevention

❖ **Beyond Blue** is an Australian mental health and wellbeing support organisation. They provide support programs to address issues related to depression, suicide, anxiety disorders and other related mental illnesses.

Ph. 1300 22 4636

❖ **Carers Foundation Australia** helps carers to respond to extremely difficult situations in healthier ways. **Important: CFA does *not* provide crisis intervention or counselling services.**

+61 7 3289 4552 | 0401291450
info@thecarersfoundation.org

❖ **Lifeline Australia** is a non-profit organisation that provides free 24-hour telephone crisis support in Australia. Volunteer crisis supporters provide suicide prevention services, mental health support and emotional assistance, not only via telephone but also face-to-face and online.

24/7 Crisis Lifeline: Ph 13 11 14

❖ **Roses in the Ocean** exists to save lives and to reduce emotional distress and pain. We do this by informing, influencing and enhancing suicide prevention through the lived experience and supporting organisations to effectively and meaningfully engage lived experience expertise. **Important: Roses in the Ocean does *not* provide crisis intervention or counselling services.**

https://rosesintheocean.com.au/

❖ **Suicide Call Back Service 24/7** is a free telephone and counselling service for anyone affected by suicide. It might sound strange, but you can call back and speak to the same person each time.

Ph 1300 659 467

❖ **White Wreath Association** fights for positive changes of Action Against Suicide and speaks out about Mental illness and Suicide within the wider community nationally. **Important: does *not* provide crisis intervention or counselling services.**

www.whitewreath.org.au

**In New Zealand:**

❖ **Depression Helpline:**

https://depression.org.nz
Ph: 0800 111 757 | Text: 4202

❖ **Lifeline Aotearoa:**

Ph: 0800 543 354 | Text: 4357
Crisis hotline: 0508 828 865
https://www.lifeline.org.nz/suicide-prevention

❖ **NZ Suicide Prevention Trust:**

Ph: 0508 435 728
http://www.reigningingrace.org/nzspt.htm

❖ **STAROS Affected by Suicide Support Group:**

http://www.staros.org.nz
Ph: 0272 864 071 | 0276 843 033

❖ **Suicide Support "ACROSS":**

http://www.across.org.nz
Ph: 0800 227 677

### In America:

❖   Call 1-800-273-8255
https://suicidepreventionlifeline.org/

### In Canada:

❖   Call 1-833-456-4566
https://www.canada.ca/en/public-health/services/suicide-prevention/warning-signs.html

❖   **Canada Suicide Prevention Services:**

https://www.crisisservicescanada.ca/en/

### In the United Kingdom:

❖   Call 116 123

https://www.nhs.uk/conditions/suicide/

❖   **CALM:** A web-based support movement.

Ph: 0800 58 58 58 (every day, 5pm – midnight)
https://www.thecalmzone.net/

❖   **Grassroots:**

https://www.prevent-suicide.org.uk/

❖   **National Suicide Prevention Alliance:**

https://www.nspa.org.uk/

❖   **Papyrus Suicide helpline:** a great support for youth.

Ph: 0800 068 41 41 (every day, 9am – midnight)

Made in the USA
Monee, IL
04 May 2021